THE WORLD'S BEST
ASIAN NOODLE RECIPES

THE WORLD'S BEST
ASIAN NOODLE RECIPES

Foreword by
Ian Kittichai

Race Point
PUBLISHING

A division of Book Sales, Inc.
276 Fifth Avenue, Suite 206
New York, New York 10001

RACE POINT PUBLISHING and the distinctive Race Point Publishing logo are trademarks of
Book Sales, Inc.

© 2013 by The Book Shop, Ltd.
7 Peter Cooper Road
New York, NY 10010

This 2013 edition published by Race Point Publishing
by arrangement with The Book Shop, Ltd.

RECIPE SELECTION Kirsten Hall
FOOD EDITOR AND WRITER Susan Sulich
DESIGNER, PHOTO RESEARCHER Tim Palin Creative

ISBN-13: 978-1-937994-20-4

Printed in China

2 4 6 8 10 9 7 5 3 1

www.racepointpub.com

TABLE OF CONTENTS

THE WORLD'S BEST ASIAN NOODLE RECIPES

ACKNOWLEDGMENTS

Special thanks from Kirsten Hall and The Book Shop, Ltd to:

Chef Ian Kittichai, who provided his wonderful recipes and the foreword for our book. We also appreciate the support we received from Sarah Chang and Ian's whole team, especially Chef Paul Kinny (Executive Chef, Intercontinental Marine Drive Hotel, Mumbai, India), Chef Pavita Sae-Chao, and Chef Wittawat Jermsurawong.

Tak Kubodera, who not only obtained recipes from noodle houses on the other side of the world, but personally went to meet with the chefs and tasted and photographed their wonderful contributions.

Lisann Araujo, Yvette Garfield, Nicholas Miles, Andrea Rademan, and Nikki Sato, our tireless recipe scouts for their time and efforts in collecting the recipes in this book, which successfully represent a wide range of styles, ethnicities, and chefs.

Theresa Christensen for keeping track of the many pieces as they came flying in from all over the world.

All of the chefs who were generous enough to share their recipes with us.

All photographs were provided by the respective chefs unless otherwise indicated below:

MIXA/Getty Images: Front Cover; Data Co Ltd./Getty Images: Endpapers, 18; Ant Photography/Getty Images: 87; Dave King/Getty Images: 104; Foodcollection/Getty Images: 149; Martin Harvey/Getty Images: 165; Willie Nash/Getty Images: 187; Anna Esposto/Getty Images: 207; artparadigm/Getty Images: 219; MIB Pictures/Getty Images: 233; Greg Thomson/Getty Images: 243; Bellamy Hunt/Getty Images: 281

Thinkstock: Backgrounds throughout, 3, 10-11, 13, 14-15, 16-17, 19, 20-21, 22-23, 36, 45, 55, 59, 61, 67, 69, 72, 79, 93, 95, 99, 101, 102, 114, 123, 125, 126, 131, 167, 195, 197, 199, 205, 213, 215, 228, 241, 260, 271, 273, 275, 277, 278

Christie Uy: 122, 184

Imadake/Mineho Okunishi: Back Cover

FOREWORD

Noodles are beloved all throughout Asia and now throughout the world. I grew up in a big Thai-Chinese family in Bangkok, Thailand where noodles were a significant part of my life. Not only did my family regularly eat noodles as part of our everyday cuisine, but we also had a green grocery where we made and sold noodles and noodle dishes. My family also made Chinese-style egg noodles to sell to other noodle shops and restaurants. Our own specialty hot dish was a braised pork shank over wide flat rice noodles (a version of this dish can be found in my Street Style Noodles recipe on page 130). It was here my culinary training began at a very young age. I remember learning how to make noodles when I was eight or nine years old while working in my family's shop. We would make huge batches of egg noodles at one time, using up to 100 chicken eggs to get the noodles a beautiful yellow hue. (See recipe, page 17.) It was my responsibility to crack each egg into a large bowl, being careful to avoid pieces of shells and bad eggs from getting into the mix.

There are a wide variety of noodles and each country has its own specialty styles and dishes—for example, Japan has udon and buckwheat soba noodles, Thailand has boat noodle soup, and Malaysia has laksa. The noodle is actually thousands of years old and originates from China. In Chinese culture the noodle is a symbol of longevity and it is typically eaten for birthday celebrations and New Year celebrations. Given this symbolism, it is considered unlucky to cut up a strand of noodle. The Japanese also eat noodles to ring in the New Year.

Noodles are a highly functional ingredient—they can be a very fast on-the-go snack, like an instant cup of noodles or ramen, to a staple for simple family meals like stewed pork or beef over noodles, to something much more sophisticated and elegant. In this wonderful book you will find recipes that fall into the categories of all of the aforementioned types of dishes.

From personal and professional experience I can tell you that the best way to get familiar with the versatility of the noodle and ingredients that go with it in this book is to try the recipes and experiment. Noodles are fun to cook with and to eat, so get creative and do not be afraid to try something new or make a bit of a mess—it's the best way to learn!

Keep Cooking!

Chef Ian Kittichai

INTRODUCTION

Noodles could very well be the answer to that age-old question: "If you were stranded on a desert island and could only have one food with you, what would it be?" Every culture has them and regardless of country or ethnicity, noodles always seem to be equated with comfort. What distinguishes Asian noodle dishes from Italian or American pasta dishes is, first, the wide variety of ingredients used to make the noodles. There are egg noodles but there are also Chinese rice noodles, Japanese noodles made from buckwheat flour, noodles made with lotus leaf and acorn powder, and even noodles made from bean sprouts. Noodles become the palette on which many flavors can be painted. The other standout factor about Asian noodle dishes, as the recipes in this book show, is the type and use of ingredients that go into the dishes. While there are some sauces that are mixed evenly throughout the noodles, more often there will be a number of different and strong elements—spicy, bitter, sweet, tangy, hot—that will be strategically placed to allow each individual flavor to burst through in a wonderful taste adventure. If you are already a lover of Asian noodles, you will find traditional favorites and classic recipes for many well-known noodle dishes, as well as contemporary and innovative treatments of this versatile ingredient. If you are new to Asian noodles, get out your knife, your whisk, and your wok, and hold on to your seat! You are about to embark on a culinary expedition that will lead you to new taste sensations and a wide variety of food preparations, and will leave you with many new recipes for both your daily repertoire and special entertaining— as well as a hunger to go even further in experimenting and creating Asian noodle dishes.

ASIAN NOODLES LONG AGO AND TODAY

For centuries a culinary dispute about who invented the noodle raged between Italy and China. An archeological find in 2005, however, settled the argument when a 4,000-year-old bowl of noodles was discovered, beautifully preserved, at a dig in northwestern China.

In addition to being a staple in all Asian kitchens, noodles are also an art form when made by the hands of practiced masters. Although today most noodles are made by machine, ancient techniques of pulling and twisting noodles deftly and with great speed can still be witnessed in Asian countries. There are even competitions using recipes handed down from generation to generation. In many areas noodles are still dried in age-old ways, hung out like long clotheslines in the sun or set on bamboo mats (that's the reason why rice sheets often have wavy lines on the surface).

Asian noodles are basically made by five different techniques:

Cut—dough is rolled out flat and then can be folded or left in a single layer and cut to the desired widths

Kneaded—dough is pressed and rolled on a hard surface and then small pieces are molded into shapes

Peeled—dough is shaped into a long loaf and then small pieces or strips are cut or pinched off and dropped directly into boiling water or broth to cook

Pulled—dough is rolled into a long snake-like coil and then stretched and folded over and over to produce thinner and thinner strands of noodles

Extruded—dough is forced through a press with holes in it to form noodle strands

Fresh Noodles vs. Dry

Some noodles are available in both fresh and dried forms. For many recipes, chefs will specify what type of noodle should be used. Many noodle dishes, however, are pretty adaptable and can be made with either fresh or dried noodles and even with substituting one kind of noodle for another. If no directions are given, buy the best quality noodles you can find, keeping in mind that fresh noodles need less cooking time than dried. Feel free to experiment with different types and thicknesses to find your personal favorites.

On the following pages you will find a noodle primer, with information about the main kinds of noodles used to make the recipes in this cookbook.

SOBA NOODLES

Typically made from a blend of buckwheat and wheat flour, these noodles have an earthy, slightly nutty flavor. They are most often served cold in salads or with a dipping sauce and also in hot noodle dishes. Soba noodles are usually sold dry but this Japanese noodle can be found fresh in specialty stores. (See page 83 for a recipe to make your own fresh soba noodles.) Usually gray or brown, there is also a pink variety made with ume and a green variety that is made using green tea (see Seared Atlantic Salmon with Green Tea Soba Noodles in a Ginger Lime Broth, page 66, and Cold Green Tea Noodles with Sesame Sauce, page 248).

RAMEN NOODLES

While often thought of as that college student staple—a dried block of instant noodles in a cellophane wrapper—ramen is actually available fresh as well. These thin noodles are wheat based and sometimes contain eggs. In addition to the instant variety (which have been deep fried before they are dried), they are sold fresh, dried, and frozen in straight rods as well as the familiar crinkly block. Boil ramen noodles before adding to a dish.

How to Make Ramen Noodles

This recipe makes two portions (up to two big bowls of noodles for a soup dish).

3/4 cup/75 g bread flour (may substitute all-purpose flour), plus additional flour for rolling/stretching

1 tsp baking soda

3/4 tsp salt (or to taste)

1 egg

1 tbsp water (depending on flour and humidity)

1. Mix the flour, baking soda, and salt in a bowl. Add the egg and water to the dry ingredients, mixing well, until all ingredients are combined together.

2. Once mixed, place dough onto a clean counter (or large cutting board) and begin kneading. It should feel a little stiffer than bread dough. Knead for at least 5-6 minutes, until the dough doesn't feel super sticky and is more or less dry. When it is the right consistency, you should be able to lift your hand from the dough fairly easily. If it's too sticky, add a little more flour and knead it in. If it's too dry, add water a few drops at a time.

3. The dough will need to rest before it gets stretched, otherwise it will not make nice thin noodles. Wrap dough in a damp cloth and leave for at least 30 minutes in warm/hot environments, and up to 2 hours in a cold environment.

4. Remove dough ball and sprinkle some flour generously over the dough. Take a rolling pin or roller and start stretching it. (Ideally you want to roll/stretch dough to large rectangular shape.)

5. If you can, get it to about ⅛-inch/3-mm thickness.. If dough is overly sticky, add a bit more dry flour to it.

6. If dough feels too elastic in nature and seems to be shrinking back into its original shape, simply allow it to rest for a few minutes, untouched.

7. If you haven't been working on a cutting board, now's the time to transfer the sheet of dough to a cutting board so you don't damage your counter. Liberally spread flour on the surface, because if dough starts sticking when you cut it, the ramen will be ruined. Fold dough two times in the same direction, each time spreading flour on the surface, and eventually dust some flour on the top. All that additional loose surface flour will wash off when noodles are boiled, plus the starch flour in the water will help keep the noodles together during the boiling process.

8. Once dough has been folded over itself, start cutting it into thin strips. A long flat (non-serrated) knife works best, but any knife will work if it is long enough.

9. When in doubt, spread some more flour on top of the noodles and/or on surface below the dough. You don't want the dough to get sticky! Once you have a pile of cut noodles, fluff them with your fingers to unfold them. Toss them around with some more flour, but just be careful not to break the noodles.

10. Bring a medium-large pot of water to a rolling boil. Once the water boils, salt it liberally, and sprinkle the noodles into the water, keeping the heat high. Do not dump the noodles in or they will stick. Mix the noodles around delicately with a wood spoon or chopsticks for the first minute.

11. As long as the water is hot enough, they should start floating.

12. Boil the noodles for about 4 minutes, depending on how thin they are cut. The best doneness test is to just taste the noodles and drain them when they're barely soft enough.

Recipe by Chef Matthew Gray of Hawaii Food Tours

EGG NOODLES

This category includes noodles of all shapes and sizes: round, flat, wide, thin. Egg noodles are made with wheat flour and are yellow because of the eggs. They are rich and chewy and are used in soups, lo mein, chow mein, and other noodle dishes. Sometimes they are fried. They can be found dried and fresh—the dried ones have to be boiled and the fresh ones can be cooked right in dishes with liquid. Very thin egg noodles are called **wonton noodles** and are frequently used in soups. **Shanghai noodles** are a thicker egg noodle that also contains semolina flour. Shanghai noodles are usually sold fresh but can be found dried in long rods as well. These noodles do require boiling. They are popular for stir-fry dishes.

How to Make Egg Noodles

Serves 2-4

2 cups/200 g all purpose flour

1 tsp salt

3 large eggs

1 tbsp vegetable or canola oil

1. Combine flour and salt in a large bowl. Mix well and crack the eggs into the middle of it.

2. Use a fork to beat eggs. Add the oil and gradually start incorporating the flour into the egg/oil mix. Keep stirring and pulling in more flour until a solid dough forms. The dough will be sticky and smooth.

3. Cover with plastic wrap and chill for at least 30 minutes.

4. Roll the dough into a thin sheet. Use knife or cutting rollers to cut the dough into thin noodles until all the dough is used.

5. Keep noodles in a dry plastic bag or airtight container, and set aside in refrigerator overnight or for up to several days.

Recipe by Ian Kittichai

UDON NOODLES

These fat Japanese noodles are made from wheat flour and are served hot in soups and stir fries as well as cold with dipping sauce. They have a chewy, but tender, springy texture, which comes from repeated rolling and kneading. Udon is sold fresh and dried and both varieties need to be boiled.

How to Make Udon Noodles

Serves 2

3 cups/300 g all-purpose flour

3 tbsp potato starch

⅔ cup/150 ml water

½ tbsp salt

1¼ tsp grapeseed oil

1. Combine all above ingredients in a bowl and mix well to form a dough.

2. On the counter, knead the dough for several minutes. Roll the dough out into a rectangular shape and fold the dough twice (like making puff pastry) and roll the dough out again. Repeat the "roll and fold" several times. The more you repeat the process, the springier the dough will be and the better consistency it will have.

3. Put the kneaded dough into a sealable plastic storage bag and seal it. Let the dough rest at room temperature for 24 hrs. *IT MUST BE ROOM TEMPERATURE.

4. Dust the counter with flour and roll out the dough to a thickness from ⅛- to ¼-inch/3- to 5-mm. Fold the dough into half, sprinkling with enough flour first so that the two sides do not stick to each other. Cut the dough with a knife to size (about the width of linguine noodles).

5. Spread the noodles out so they do not stick to each other.

6. Bring a pot of water to a boil and cook the noodles for 10 to 12 minutes. Drain and serve in prepared broth.

Time saving tip: You can make the dough ahead and cook the noodles, drain, rinse in cold water, and drain again. Then divide them into single servings and freeze the portions.

Recipe from Catherine Shaffer, Contemporary Korean Kitchen

RICE NOODLES

The general category "rice noodles" encompasses a large number of noodles. They come in a variety of thicknesses but are all made with rice flour. Very thin ones are called **vermicelli**. They are white and translucent, tender to the bite, and mild in flavor. Similar in texture and appearance to cellophane noodles, they also only need to be soaked, not boiled. Other common varieties of rice noodles are **rice sticks** (which come in thicker and wider widths than vermicelli), **pad Thai noodles**, and **rice paper** (see page 26 for a recipe to make your own). Rice noodles are generally sold dried. Brown rice noodles are also available. **Khanom jeen noodles** are yet another variety and they are made from fermented rice.

CELLOPHANE NOODLES

Also called glass noodles because they're nearly transparent, these very thin, slippery noodles are made from mung bean starch (hence other names: bean threads, soybean vermicelli). They have a mild flavor and are often used in soups, salads and spring rolls. Sold dried, in bundles, they only need to be soaked in warm water to use or they can be cooked directly in soups and sauces.

TOFU NOODLES

A welcome variety for people on gluten-free and low-carb diets, tofu noodles come in a wide variety of shapes and sizes from long spaghetti to little knots. Made from compressed tofu, they are high in protein and other nutrients. They are available fresh, frozen, and dried. Fresh tofu noodles need to be rinsed and dried before using, while dried ones will have to be soaked first. Also in this category are **shiritaki noodles**, which are made from a gelatinous substance that comes from the Japanese yam plant. Slightly rubbery and with no taste of their own, these translucent noodles will pick up the flavors of whatever they are cooked in. They can be cooked right in soups or soaked before using.

To make your own tofu noodles, start with "firm" or "extra firm" tofu. Cut long, matchstick-sized strips of the tofu and toss with a neutral oil. Then bake at 350°F/177°C for 15-20 minutes. (The oven-drying makes the tofu even firmer and allows for easier cooking.) Noodles are then ready to be used in a stir-fry or other noodle dish.

Tofu noodle directions by Chef Matthew Gray of Hawaii Food Tours

POTATO NOODLES

A Korean favorite is the **sweet potato noodle**, which, as its name implies, is made from sweet potato starch. Translucent, thin, and slippery, they resemble cellophane noodles in appearance but they are a little thicker and tougher in texture. **Sujebi** is a noodle made from white potatoes and wheat flour (see page 57 for a recipe). Both of these varieties require boiling.

SOMEN NOODLES

Similar to udon, the defining characteristic of these Japanese wheat noodles is that they are very thin (less than $\frac{1}{20}$ inch/1.3 mm in diameter). They make a refreshing summer dish served cold with dipping sauce, as well as hearty fare in the winter when added to hot soups. Somen noodles are found in Asian groceries, dried in long bundles.

OIL NOODLES

As their name implies, these noodles use oil in their dough. They are made with wheat flour and sometimes eggs. Oil noodles are usually very thin but need to be boiled before using. They can be eaten hot or cold and are often found in soups.

How to Make Oil Noodles

Serves 2

3 cups/300 g all-purpose flour

1 cup/240 ml boiling water

½ cup/120 ml cold water

2 tbsp oil

1 tsp salt

1. Mix the flour with the boiling water.

2. Then add the cold water, oil and salt.

3. Roll out into a thin sheet and then use a pasta machine or a sharp knife to cut into very thin noodles.

Recipe by Theresa Lin

SPECIALTY NOODLES

Other varieties of noodles used in Asian cooking are made using special flours or ingredients for flavor and texture. Two found in this cookbook are **acorn noodles** (see page 202) and **lotus leaf noodles** (see page 216), made from their namesake ingredients. Other specialty noodle additions include mushrooms, tomatoes, and other vegetables, seafood, or seasonings.

SEAFOOD

CHINESE LASAGNA

Homemade lasagna noodles with layers of shrimp and black beans
alternating with sizzling vegetables

Hawaii Food Tours

www.HawaiiFoodTours.com

Chef Matthew Gray

Chef Matthew Gray

Gray, a former professional chef, has cooked for movie stars and rock and roll bands. He was the food writer and restaurant critic for Hawaii's largest newspaper for several years before starting Hawaii Food Tours, voted the best tour in Hawaii for the past two years.

Serves 8-10

For Rice Noodles:

You will need a steamer to make these.

¾ cup/115 g rice flour

1 tbsp tapioca flour

1 tbsp cornstarch

¼ tsp salt

1 tbsp oil

¾ cup/180 ml cold water

½ cup/120 ml boiling water

* You may wish to add some thinly sliced green onion to batter.

1. Spray two 8-in/20-cm pie pans with vegetable oil. Bring steamer to a rolling boil.

2. In a medium bowl, combine the rice flour, tapioca flour, cornstarch, salt, and oil.

3. Add cold water and stir until smooth. Stir in the boiling water and chopped green onion.

4. Reduce the heat for the steamer so that the water is barely bubbling.

5. Give the batter a quick stir, then ladle ¼ cup/60 ml of the batter into a pie pan tilting the pan to spread the batter evenly.

6. Cover and steam for about 5-6 minutes, or until the sheet has cooked through.

7. Place the hot pan into a dish of cold water for a few minutes to cool down, or place on a rack in front of a blowing fan for several minutes.

8. Use a flat spatula to loosen the sheet along one edge, then roll it up loosely. Transfer to a plate.

9. Repeat with the remaining batter and pie tins, cleaning and oiling the pans each time, and replenishing the simmering water in steamer as necessary.

10. Noodles are now ready to be used in the lasagna.

For Choy Sum Sizzle Layer:

1 large bunch choy sum

½ tsp salt

½ lb/230 g fresh snow peas, washed, stringy parts removed, julienned

8-10 fresh water chestnuts, peeled and sliced thinly

1 tbsp oyster sauce

1 tsp rice vinegar

1 tbsp peanut oil

1 tbsp dark sesame oil

1. Remove majority of stems from choy sum, cut crosswise into 4 equally-sized pieces, and wash thoroughly. (I submerge in big bowl of cold water several times to remove dirt.)

2. Bring a pot of water to a boil. Add salt to boiling water.

3. Add choy sum and simmer for about 1 minute.

4. Toss snow peas into boiling water and boil another minute.

5. Add sliced water chestnuts to pot of boiling water for 30 seconds.

6. Immediately drain veggies through a colander and place in a bowl.

7. Combine oyster sauce and rice vinegar in a small dish and pour over veggies.

8. In a small pot, heat peanut oil to smoking point, add sesame oil to this, and then carefully pour over choy sum, snow peas, and water chestnuts. It will sizzle. Toss finished dish and set aside until ready to assemble lasagna.

For Black Beans and Shrimp Layer:

For Black Bean Sauce:

3 tbsp fermented black beans, rinsed well, then mashed

2 tbsp naturally fermented soy sauce

2 tsp sugar

2 tsp oyster sauce

2 tsp cornstarch mixed into 2 tsp of water

3 cloves of garlic, finely minced

1 cup/240 ml low-sodium chicken stock

Mix all ingredients together in a bowl until well combined.

2 tbsp bacon fat/drippings

2 lbs/900 g shrimp (16-20 size is good), peeled, deveined, washed, dried, and sliced horizontally

1 tbsp unsalted butter, softened

1. Over high heat, pre-heat large skillet for 1-2 minutes.

2. Add bacon fat/drippings to pan and get them blazing hot.

3. Add shrimp to pan in single layer for one minute.

4. Turn shrimp over and immediately add black bean sauce.

5. Continue to sauté for one more minute.

6. Turn heat off.

7. Add softened butter and toss or stir throughout.

To assemble: Place one lasagna noodle in a deep, round metal or ceramic dish. Add a layer of Black Beans and Shrimp, then another noodle and a layer of Choy Sum Sizzle. Continue alternating noodles and fillings, until fillings and noodles are all used.

Serve immediately.

CRAB RAMEN WITH ASIAN TRUFFLE BROTH

Truffle oil and truffle butter combined with
dungeness crab create a rich and elegant dish

Seafood Restaurant & Sushi Bar

Sansei

Kihei Town Center
1881 South Kihei Road, #KT-116
Kihei, HI 96753
(808) 879-0004

Three other locations:
Waikiki Beach, Oahu
Kapalua Resort, Maui
Waikoloa Beach Resort, Hawaii

Cuisine: Contemporary sushi and new wave
Asian dishes

Chef Dave "DK" Kodama

In Japanese, the word *sansei*
refers to "third generation,"
and founder D.K. Kodama
felt that this was a fitting
name for a restaurant inspired
by Japanese tradition, but
serving contemporary
interpretations of sushi and
Asian cuisine. It is also a
reference to D.K. Kodama's
background as a third-
generation Japanese American.

Serves 1

2 cups seasoned dashi broth, heated

2½-3 oz/70-85g fresh ramen noodles

2 tbsp truffle butter, recipe follows or purchased

¼ cup/50g cooked crab meat,
    Dungeness preferred

1 tbsp fresh cilantro, coarsely chopped

1 tbsp Thai basil, coarsely chopped

1 tbsp green onions, sliced thin

2-3 jalapeño rings, thinly sliced

2-3 drops white truffle oil

For Truffle Butter:

4 oz (1 stick)/113g unsalted butter, softened

1 tbsp white truffle oil

1 tbsp black truffle peelings, minced

Kosher salt, to taste

Whip butter until creamy. Blend in truffle oil.
Fold in the truffle peelings and season to taste
with salt. Makes ¼ cup/60 g. Store refrigerated.

1.   Heat seasoned dashi broth to a simmer.

2.   Meanwhile, bring a small pot of water to a
boil. Loosen ramen noodles and place into
a pasta strainer basket. Immerse noodles
into the boiling water and let cook for
approximately 2 minutes or until al dente.

3.   Remove noodles and drain off excess water.
Place into serving bowl, add truffle butter
and toss to coat noodles.

4.   Top noodles with the crab meat.

5.   Ladle hot dashi broth over noodles and
garnish with cilantro, Thai basil, green
onions, and jalapeños. Drizzle with truffle
oil and serve.

Chef Dave "DK" Kodama

Dave Kodama, known simply as "DK," now
owns and operates nine restaurants on three
Hawaiian islands. This "local boy" from
'Aiea, O'ahu, opened his first Sansei Seafood
Restaurant & Sushi Bar in Kapalua, Maui,
sixteen years ago. Kodama is one of sixteen
children and was following in his father's
footsteps as a civil engineering major at the
University of Hawai'i when the bug bit. In 1979
he became the first of his clan to venture off
to the Mainland into the restaurant business.
He spent three years in Seattle and a decade in
Aspen where he learned the art of making sushi
and worked for an upscale caterer. During the
off-season at the ski resort, Kodama traveled
throughout the United States, Mexico, and the
Caribbean to introduce his palate to a world of
new flavors and culinary styles.

CRISPY PRAWN COCOONS

This very original presentation calls for wrapping the pasta
around the shrimp and then deep-frying

M.Y. CHINA

M.Y. China
845 Market Street, Level 4
San Francisco, CA 94103
(415) 580-3001

Cuisine: Chinese

Chef Martin Yan

M.Y. China offers authentic Chinese cuisine
in a modern experience. Inspired by Chef
Martin Yan and his years of teaching the art
of Chinese cuisine, a full exhibition kitchen
brings the ancient art of the wok, hand-pulled
noodles, and dim sum to light.

Chef Martin Yan

The celebrated host of over 3,000 cooking
shows broadcast worldwide, Martin Yan enjoys
distinction as a certified Master Chef, a highly
respected food consultant, a cooking instructor,
and a prolific author.

Serves 4

8 raw jumbo prawns, peeled and deveined with
    tail shell on

¼ tsp salt

⅛ tsp ground white pepper

4 oz/113 g fresh, uncooked Asian angel hair
    noodles

¼ cup/60 ml prepared sweet and sour sauce

2 tbsp chili garlic sauce

1 tsp fresh lime juice

Vegetable oil for deep-frying

1. Season prawns with salt and pepper. Set
    aside to marinate for 5 minutes.

2. Untangle noodles and divide into 8
    equal portions. Wind one portion of
    the noodles around each prawn so it is
    completely covered; press noodles to
    form a tight wrap.

3. To make dipping sauce, combine sweet
    and sour sauce, chili garlic sauce, and
    lime juice together in a small bowl. Set
    aside.

4. Pour oil into a wok to a depth of 2 in/5
    cm. Heat over medium-high heat until
    temperature reaches 350° F/177° C.
    Deep-fry prawns, a few at a time, turning
    once, until golden brown, 6-7 minutes.
    Remove and drain on paper towels. Serve
    with dipping sauce on the side.

DEEP FRIED CRAB FAT NOODLE

Rich noodles hidden in a spring roll wrapper and topped with shrimp

The Sultry Chef

Mezza Norte Trinoma
Quezon City, Philippines
63 2 917 422 2221

Cuisine: Asian Mediterranean

Chef Ivory Yat

Chef Ivory Yat

Ivory Yat placed third in the
Master Chef Philippines
competition. This recipe is
the dish she created in twenty
minutes. In addition to launching
her restaurant, she is pursuing a
culinary diploma at the Center
for Asian Culinary Studies.

Serves 2

4 oz/100 g rice noodles (pre-soaked)

1 tsp fennel seeds

4 cloves of garlic, minced

2 shallots, minced

1 tbsp butter

1 tbsp olive oil

8 shrimp, sliced in half

4 tbsp crab fat or crab paste

½ cup/120 ml shrimp broth

1 cup/240 ml coconut milk

Spring roll wrappers or shell

Oil for frying

Springs of spring onion, for garnish

For Baby Squid Adobo:

6 cloves garlic, sliced

2 shallots

3 bay leaves

1 piece dried chili

½ cup/120 ml olive oil

4 oz/100 g baby squid, cleaned

⅓ cup/80 ml balsamic vinegar

Worcestershire sauce, to taste

For Asian Gremolata:

Sprig of wansoy or cilantro, minced

Sprig of spring onion, minced

2 cloves garlic, minced

1 lemon, zest and juice

1 lime, zest and juice

1 tbsp fish sauce (optional)

1 tbsp sugar

1. Soak rice noodles in lukewarm water with the fennel seeds. Strain when noodles are soft.

2. In a pan, sauté garlic and shallots in butter and olive oil. Add shrimp and crab paste and sauté until paste gives up its oil.

3. Add shrimp broth and coconut milk. Then mix in rice noodles and turn off heat.

4. In another pan make the baby squid adobo. Sauté garlic slices, shallots, bay leaves, and chili in olive oil until fragrant, and garlic has turned golden.

5. Add squid and cook for 30 seconds. Add in balsamic vinegar and Worcestershire sauce. Reduce, and set aside.

6. Take a sheet of spring roll wrapper and lay it on a flat surface, put a couple of spoonfuls of your crabfat noodle in the center, and wrap it diagonally like a parcel. Seal it with a flour and water paste.

7. In a large pan heat oil and fry noodle parcels one at a time until golden. There should be an air pocket at the middle. Strain in a colander lined with paper towels.

8. To make the gremolata, mix wansoy, spring onion, garlic, lemon zest and lime zest in a bowl. Squeeze in lemon and lime juice. Add in fish sauce and sugar. Mix all together. Chill.

9. Put a layer of shrimp and then half of the baby squid adobo on the bottom of each of two plates. Place a noodle parcel on top and the Asian gremolata. Garnish with sprigs of spring onions and remaining shrimp. Enjoy!

DRUNKEN NOODLES WITH SHRIMP

Tofu noodles are the base of this healthy dish

House Foods

Chef Mai Pham

Mai Pham is the chef/owner of the nationally acclaimed Lemon Grass and Star Ginger restaurants in Sacramento, California. A recognized expert on Asian cuisine and industry leader, Chef Pham is known for her innovative, fresh take on Vietnamese, Thai and other Southeast Asian cooking. The author of several award-winning cookbooks as well as host of the TV Food Network *My Country, My Kitchen* series, she's a frequent guest chef instructor at The Culinary Institute of America. Chef Pham's recipes feature homestyle foods that she grew up with in Vietnam and Thailand, including dishes such as Mom's Catfish in Claypot. Chef Mai partnered with House Foods Tofu to create a childhood street food favorite, Drunken Noodles with Shrimp.

Serves 3-5

3 (8 oz/230 g) packages of House Foods Tofu
    Shirataki noodles, spaghetti shaped

½ lb/230 g shrimp

1 tbsp cornstarch

⅛ cup/30 ml water

2 tbsp vegetable oil

¼ cup/20 g shallots, diced (or other onion)

2 cloves of garlic, minced

½ yellow onion, thinly sliced

Pinch of chili flakes

¼ cup/10 g Thai basil

1 tsp fish sauce (or soy sauce)

⅛ cup/30 ml oyster sauce

⅛ cup/30 ml chicken stock

½ red bell pepper, julienned

½ cup/40 g spinach leaves

1. Rinse and drain Tofu Shirataki noodles well. Pat dry using paper towels. Put in a microwave-safe bowl and heat in microwave for 1 minute. Drain excess liquid and pat dry. Cut noodles to manageable size.

2. Combine shrimp, cornstarch, and water. Toss until evenly coated and set aside.

3. Heat oil in a large wok or tilting skillet over medium-high heat. Add shallots, garlic, onions, chili flakes, and half the basil leaves and stir until fragrant, about 3 minutes.

4. Add shrimp, cook until shrimp begins to turn pink, about 5 minutes.

5. Stir in fish sauce, oyster sauce, noodles, chicken stock, red bell peppers and spinach. Cook until vegetables are thoroughly hot.

6. Add remaining basil and if necessary add additional stock to moisten noodles.

EBI YAKISOBA

A sweet and spicy shrimp noodle dish

robata and sushi bar

Katana Robata and Sushi Bar

8439 W. Sunset Boulevard
West Hollywood, CA 90069
(323) 650-8585

Cuisine: Japanese

A favorite of celebrities from film,
television, and music, Katana has
introduced the robatayaki style
of Japanese comfort cuisine. The
restaurant features an array of
robata-style skewers, a grand sushi
bar, and special hot and cold dishes
from the kitchen and an outside
patio with view of Hollywood.

About Mirin

Mirin is a kind of rice wine but with a lower
alcohol content and higher sugar content than
sake. It is pleasing to several of the senses: Mirin
adds sweetness and has a pleasant aroma—which
is why it is often used to cover a fishy smell in
some seafood dishes—and it adds luster and
sheen to foods as well.

Serves 2

For Yakisoba Sauce:

1½ tsp Japanese rice vinegar

1 tbsp sake

1 tbsp mirin

1 tbsp tomato sauce

1 tbsp oyster sauce

2 tsp soft brown sugar

Dash of chili oil

Pinch of ground ginger

Combine all ingredients in a saucepan over high heat. Boil for about 10 minutes and then let cool for about 20 minutes.

4 oz/113 g yakisoba noodles

3 jumbo shrimp, 8-12 size

Vegetable oil for frying

4 oz/113 g mixed sautéed vegetables (carrots, cabbage, green onion)

¼ cup/60 ml olive oil

Salt and pepper, to taste

Pinch of red ginger

1.   Make the yakisoba sauce and set aside.

2.   Put noodles in boiling water for about 4 minutes; drain.

3.   Flash fry shrimp in vegetable oil for 1 minute.

4.   Sauté vegetables with olive oil, salt and pepper.

5.   Toss the noodles with the yakisoba sauce.

6.   Divide noodles between two plates and top with shrimp.

7.   Garnish with red ginger on the side.

FRESH SEA URCHIN PASTA

Flavors from the sea: clams, kelp, and sea urchin in tomato sauce with a hint of brandy

5-417-18 Makuhari chou,
Hanamigawa-ward
Chiba-shi, Chiba prefecture
Japan
81 043 304 5020

Cuisine: Italian

Chef Kazuyoshi Takaura

This eclectic food destination offers diners a wide variety of options to suit their taste moods: It is a restaurant, a deli and a wine shop all in one.

Chef Kazuyoshi Takaura

Takaura's stunningly original menu is the result of his diverse path in culinary instruction. He first trained in a famous Italian restaurant in Tokyo, then later went on to become a sommelier. This accounts for perfect pairings of wine with the varied items on the menu at his restaurant.

Serves 4

For Clam and Kelp Broth:
1 qt/1 L water
1½ oz/40 g kelp
1 tbsp butter
1 medium-size shallot, thinly sliced
2¼ lb/1 kg clams
¾ cup/200 ml white wine

1. Put water into a bowl. Add kelp and let it rest overnight to make kelp water.

2. Melt butter in a stockpot.

3. Add shallot and stir over medium low heat.

4. When you start to smell the shallot, add clams and white wine and cover. Turn up heat to high.

5. When the clams open, add kelp water and bring to a boil. Remove from heat and set aside.

2 tbsp olive oil
2 cloves of garlic, minced
1 chili pepper
2 cups/400 ml clam and kelp broth
Splash of brandy
4 tbsp tomato puree
½ lb/200 g fresh sea urchin
12 oz/320 g spaghetti
Salt

1. Put olive oil and minced garlic into a pan and stir over low heat.

2. When you start to smell garlic, add chili pepper, 2 cups/400 ml broth, and brandy and boil down to half.

3. Add tomato puree and half of the sea urchin and dissolve into the sauce.

4. Boil spaghetti and drain.

5. Add spaghetti and the rest of the sea urchin and season with salt to taste.

GREEDY ELEPHANT PAD THAI

Homemade Pad Thai sauce adds unbeatable flavor to this shrimp and noodle dish

Serves 2

Vegetable oil for stir-frying

8-10 king prawns or 2-4 super king prawns

2 eggs

8 oz/230 g Thai rice noodles

Pad Thai sauce (recipe below)

⅓ cup/50 g crushed or roughly chopped
    peanuts

3 cups/300 g fresh bean sprouts

1 spring onion, sliced

Wedges of lime

1 tsp chili flakes

For Pad Thai Sauce:

3 red peppers

1 clove of garlic

¼ cup warm water

1-3 tsp. tomato ketchup

¾ Tbsp. tamarind paste

2 Tbsp. fish sauce + more to taste

3 Tbsp. dried sugarcane

Pinch of salt

Blend the red peppers and garlic in a food processor. Place in a saucepan with the water and bring to a boil. Then add ketchup and boil for 5 minutes. Add tamarind paste, fish sauce, sugarcane, and salt and boil for 15 minutes more. Remove from heat and set aside.

1. Heat a wok and add vegetable oil. When the oil is hot, add king prawns and the eggs and stir until cooked.

2. Add the fresh noodles and stir them all together.

3. Stir in your freshly made pad thai sauce. Then add the crushed peanuts, bean sprouts and spring onions.

4. Serve with a wedge of lime and chili flakes on the side.

THE
GREEDY ELEPHANT
THAI CUISINE · WEYBRIDGE

The Greedy Elephant

57 Queens Road
Weybridge KT13 9UQ
England
44 1932 856 779

Cuisine: Thai

Chef Arm Chaiyapruk

Thai food is all about contrasting and complementing tastes, such as hot, sour, sweet, and spicy, with every dish busting with flavor. At Greedy Elephant, every dish is prepared fresh to order, so whether you like your food mild or blow-your-brains-out hot, all dishes are prepared exactly as customers wish.

Chef Arm Chaiyapruk

Head chef Arm Chaiyapruk, who prepared the wok-based magic in the picture on the facing page, spent ten years running Kampan restaurant in Southsea before bringing that experience and flair to his new flagship restaurant in Weybridge, Surrey.

HELE CRAB NOODLE SOUP

Many complex flavors combine to make this crab soup

Anantara
MUI NE
RESORT & SPA

Shi Yuan Restaurant

No. 6 Xiaodonghai Road
Hedong District, Sanya, Hainan
China 572000
86 898 8888 5088

Cuisine: Thai

Chef Anak Koonmart

Encounter the fresh flavors of Sanya, cooked right in front of you by our expert chefs. Shi Yuan or "Origin" is an interactive dining adventure, designed to bring the fresh taste of the landscape to your plate.

Serves 1

For the Broth:

2 cups/475 ml water

2 stalks lemongrass, sliced

4-6 kaffir lime leaves, torn in half

2 cloves garlic

1 piece coriander root

2 medium-sized tomatoes, quartered

3 tbsp soy sauce

½ tbsp chili paste (or to taste)

½ tbsp salt

1 whole crab

5 oz/150 g rice noodles

3 leaves of green Chinese lettuce

Small handful bean sprouts

1 long bean, sliced

Garnish:

Coriander leaves

1 tsp sliced deep-fried shallot

½ of a hard-boiled egg

1 tsp chopped shrimp, lightly cooked in chili oil for 5 minutes

Condiments:

Chili powder

Chinese pickle

Lime

Soy sauce

1. Make the broth: In a large pot, bring water, lemongrass, kaffir leaves, garlic, coriander, and tomato to a rapid boil for 5 minutes to let the ingredients discharge their aromatic flavors. Season with soy sauce, chili paste, and salt and simmer for 30 minutes.

2. Strain broth and return to pot. Bring back to a boil.

3. Drop in whole crab and cook for 5 minutes. Turn off heat.

4. Prepare the noodles: Bring a pot of water to a boil and add rice noodles. Cook until done, approximately 5 minutes. Drain and rinse in cold water.

5. Place noodles in a large bowl.

6. Add lettuce, bean sprouts and long bean.

7. Pour broth and crab over top.

8. Sprinkle on some coriander leaves. Top with shallot, egg and shrimp.

9. Serve condiments on the side.

HOT GARLIC SHRIMP ON STIR-FRIED NOODLES

A spicy shrimp dish that packs a garlicky punch

Chef Jayanta Kishore Paul

Paul came to Los Angeles from Mumbai, where he was executive chef at a five-star hotel and caterer to royals, high-ranking politicians, industry leaders and Bollywood celebrities. His first job in the US was as opening chef at a new Beverly Hills restaurant, which, after just six months, was named Best Indian Restaurant in Los Angeles. A perfectionist about ingredients, proportions, and cooking methods, chef Paul even makes and grinds his own fresh spices. "Being a master chef," he says, "takes more than talent and training. It also requires equal part of working hard and loving what you do."

Serves 4

1½ lb/680 g tiger shrimp (large), peeled and deveined

12 oz/340 g thick egg noodles

3 tbsp soy sauce

3 tbsp chili sauce (see recipe below)

1 tsp sesame oil

1 tbsp Chinese rice wine or dry sherry

1 tsp sugar

4 tbsp peanut oil

8 cloves garlic, finely chopped

Salt and white pepper, to taste

4 green chilies, stems removed and sliced

8 sprigs cilantro, chopped

3 green onions, 2 sliced on the diagonal, 1 thinly sliced

1. Mix a little salt with the shrimp and set aside.

2. Add salt and oil to a pot of water and boil the noodles. When noodles are about 90% cooked, drain them completely and toss lightly with 1 tsp oil. Set aside until ready to use.

3. In a small bowl, mix together the soy sauce, chili sauce, sesame oil, rice wine and sugar.

4. Heat 2 tbsp peanut oil in a wok until the oil surface ripples. Tilt the wok to swirl the oil around. Add half of the chopped garlic and sauté till it is fragrant.

5. Add the noodles and stir-fry. Add salt and white pepper and mix well. Using tongs, transfer the noodles equally into four individual plates.

6. Heat remaining oil in the wok over medium-high heat. Stir-fry remaining garlic until fragrant; it will take about 25-30 seconds.

7. Add the marinated shrimp and green chilies and cook 2 minutes on each side, until shrimp are pink. Now add the chili sauce mixture and stir-fry for a minute. Add chopped cilantro and stir for one more minute so the shrimp is fully coated with the sauce.

8. Remove from the heat, divide into four equal portions, and serve on the noodles, garnished with chopped green onions.

Chili Sauce

20 dry whole red chilies

½ cup/120 ml rice vinegar

½ cup/120 ml peanut oil

Salt to taste

De-seed the red chilies and soak in rice vinegar for 30 minutes. Now put the chilies in a food processor and make a coarse paste. Heat oil in a pan, add the chili paste and stir for a minute. Add a cup of water, bring it to a boil and simmer for 15 minutes. Check salt. Remove from heat and let cool.

LEMONGRASS SHRIMP AND RICE NOODLE SALAD

This light salad has a refreshing kick of ginger and garlic

Mooncake

28 Watts Street
New York, NY 10013
(212) 219-8888

Cuisine: Pan Asian

Chef Kenny Luong

In 2003, Mooncake set out to create a new kind of Asian restaurant. Mooncake Foods breaks all traditions—no woks, no unhealthy fryers, no processed meat entrees, and no heavy heart-clogging sauces. Instead, the menu is comprised of innovative grilled, steamed, or roasted plates, salads, and sandwiches. The majority of the menu items are less than ten dollars.

Serves 4

1 lb/450 g large shrimp size (16/20 size)

2 stems of lemongrass

1 clove garlic, minced

3 tbsp sugar

1 tsp salt

1 tsp fresh minced ginger

1 tbsp minced shallots

¾ lb/340 g Vietnamese rice noodles

For the Salad:

1 head lettuce (green leaf)

2 cups/175 g mixed salad greens

¼ cup /18 g basil

1 hot pepper (jalapeño)

½ cup/150 g sliced cucumber

¼ cup/40 g cherry tomatoes

For the Dressing:

¼ cup/60 ml fish sauce

½ cup/120 ml water

1 clove garlic, minced

1 tbsp fresh minced ginger

1. Combine shrimp, lemongrass, garlic, sugar, salt, ginger, and shallots and marinate for 15 minutes.

2. Grill marinated shrimp for 2 -3 minutes on each side.

3. Boil rice noodles as instructed on the package.

4. Combine the salad mixture, and top it off with noodles and grilled shrimp.

5. Whisk all dressing ingredients together and dress salad to taste.

Chef Kenny Luong

Mooncake Foods is home-cooked Asian comfort food, as interpreted by food-loving Luong, who grew up influenced by the delicious foods of his Spanish Brooklyn neighborhood and the addictive cooking of his Chinese mother.

LINGUINE WITH CLAMS AND HOLY BASIL

Thai Holy Basil is what gives this linguine
with white clam a distinctive peppermint spiciness

Serves 2, generously

8½ oz/ 250 g linguine

2 tbsp olive oil

2 garlic cloves, peeled and sliced

1 red prik chi fah or serrano chili, sliced

14 oz/400 g fresh clams

3 oz/90 ml white wine

A large handful of Thai holy basil

Salt and freshly ground black pepper

1. In plenty of salted water, cook the linguine until it
    is al dente.

2. Meanwhile, heat a sauté pan over medium heat
    and add the olive oil.

3. When it's good and hot, add the garlic and the
    chili. Cook until the garlic is nicely golden and the
    chili has infused into the oil.

4. Add the clams and the white wine. Cover the pan
    and cook, shaking it from time to time, until the
    clams have opened.

5. Rip up the holy basil leaves and stir them into the
    clams. Season with salt and pepper, to taste.

6. Drain the linguine, then toss the pasta through the
    clams.

    If you like, you can add a few cherry tomatoes
    alongside the garlic and chili.

Kay Plunkett-Hogge

Kay Plunkett-Hogge is a cookery writer and
broadcaster, based in London.

Born and brought up in Bangkok, she spent
her childhood between two kitchens: inside for
Western food, outside for Thai.

It's an experience that has left her with a foot in
two worlds.

A former model agent in New York and London,
and a movie coordinator in Bangkok and Los
Angeles, Kay is the co-author of the best-selling
Cook Yourself Thin: Quick and Easy, *Bryn's Kitchen:
5 Brilliant Ways To Cook 20 Great Ingredients*
(both with the award-winning London chef
Bryn Williams), and *LEON: Family & Friends*
with John Vincent.

MAMA PAD KEE MAO TALAY

Basil and chili fried noodles with seafood—this free-wheeling dish comes out different everytime depending on the amounts of each ingredient you use

Servings vary

Oil, for frying

Garlic, chopped

Seafood: prawns, squids

Mama brand packet of instant noodles or spaghetti

Cabbage (optional)

Carrots (for color)

Baby corns (optional)

Mushrooms (optional)

Fish sauce

Soy sauce

Thai red/orange chilies; small and thin ones are best

Sugar

Basil leaves

1. Put oil in the pan and heat until it's hot.

2. Fry the garlic until it smells nice and turns yellow.

3. Add seafood and fry with garlic a bit.

4. Add the Mama (noodles) and fry together with the seafood..

5. Next add the vegetables and stir-fry until almost cooked.

6. Add some fish sauce and soy sauce to taste.

7. Add chilies.

8. Put a little sugar in and taste. Correct seasoning if necessary.

9. Garnish with basil leaves and serve.

Thanita Denkaew

Thanita Denkaew from Thailand is an air hostess for a Middle East airline based in Dubai. She loves traveling and enjoys eating different cuisines from around the world, but for her, her mom's cooking is still the most delicious! This recipe has been handed down in her family from generation to generation and Denkaew claims it's the best homemade Thai noodle dish in the world.

MARCO POLO NOODLE BOWL

The ginger, fish sauce and Thai basil make this an East-meets-West take
on a traditional spaghetti pomodoro with shrimp

Doc Chey's Noodle House

1424 North Highland Avenue
Atlanta, GA 30306
(404) 888-0777

Two other locations in Atlanta
and another in Asheville, NC

Cuisine: Pan-Asian

Chef Rich Chey

Doc Chey's has been serving "Great
Food . . . Good Karma" to residents of
Atlanta, Georgia, and Asheville, North
Carolina, for over sixteen years.

Chef Rich Chey

The idea for Doc Chey's came over sixteen years ago during Rich Chey's travels throughout Asia. "I really enjoyed Japan because of the Ramen houses and the role they play in society. They are the diners of Japan, where people go for delicious freshly prepared food that is affordable and served quickly." Chey and Brook Messina opened the first Doc Chey's in 1997.

Serves 2

1 tbsp vegetable oil

12 shrimp

1 tsp garlic, minced

1 cup/160 g onions, sliced

2 cups/175 g bok choy, chopped

1 cup/170 g red peppers, julienned

¾ cup/180 ml Tomato Ginger Sauce (recipe below)

12 leaves Thai basil

2 cups/180 g cooked udon noodles

1 lime wedge

1 tbsp cilantro, chopped

1. Heat oil in a pan. Cook shrimp until outside is seared and shrimp begin to turn pink. Remove from pan and set aside.

2. Add more oil to the pan, add garlic, and sauté until aromatic. Add onions, bok choy, and red peppers and sauté until bok choy begins to wilt.

3. Add tomato ginger sauce, shrimp, and Thai basil to pan and cook until sauce begins to bubble.

4. Add udon noodles and continue cooking until noodles are hot. Transfer contents to bowl and garnish with lime wedge and chopped cilantro.

For Tomato Ginger Sauce:

2 tbsp vegetable oil

1 cup/160 g onions, diced

1 tbsp garlic, minced

3 tbsp ginger, minced

1 tbsp rice vinegar

4 cups/650 g diced tomatoes (including juice)

2 cups/475 ml water

1 tsp kosher salt

2 tsp chili flakes

2 tbsp fish sauce

1. Heat oil in pot. Add onions and garlic and sauté until onions begin to caramelize.

2. Add ginger and rice vinegar and cook until vinegar is cooked off.

3. Add tomatoes, water, salt, and chili flakes. Bring contents to a boil, turn down heat, and simmer for 30 minutes.

4. Stir in fish sauce.

OMUSOBA

A Japanese variation of a shrimp omelet

Serves 1

For the Omusoba Sauce:
⅔ cup/150 ml ketchup
⅛ cup/25 ml soy sauce
⅓ cup/75 ml tonkatsu sauce
¼ cup/50 ml honey

Vegetable oil
1 egg
Half a serving of Shrimp Yakisoba
    (see page 74)

Garnish:
Mayonnaise
Aonori
Beni shouga

1. Mix the ingredients for the Omusoba
    sauce and set aside.

2. Pour a little oil in a frying pan over
    medium heat.

3. Break an egg into a bowl and beat lightly.

4. When the pan is hot, pour the egg in and
    spread it as though making a crepe. Cook
    until the egg is half done.

5. Put the half serving of shrimp yakisoba
    on a plate and place the egg on top. Use
    your hands to gently wrap the egg around
    the yakisoba.

6. Garnish with mayonnaise, omusoba
    sauce, aonori and beni shouga.

IMADAKE イマダケ

Imadake

4006 Sainte-Catherine Street West
Westmount, QC H3Z 1P2
Canada
(514) 931-8833

Cuisine: Japanese

Chef Mineho Okunishi

Imadake strives to give everyone an authentic
Japanese Izakaya experience. This extends to
every aspect of the restaurant from the recipes
and chefs to the sakes and the music. They
believe that business should not come at the
expense of the environment. All the ingredients
are environmentally sustainable. The meats and
vegetables are organic and the seafoods follow
the "OceanWise" guidelines. Imadake recycles
and uses energy-efficient appliances to lower
the impact on nature.

Chef Mineho Okunishi

Chef Mineho Okunishi has worked in various
restaurants in Japan over a period of ten years,
and has experience in different kinds of cooking,
from kaiseki to izakaya. His vision for Imadake's
menu is being able to experience the taste of
a real Japanese izakaya in Montreal without
having to set foot in Japan.

PAD WUN SEN KYUNG

Shrimp with glass noodles and red curry coconut sauce

Queen Mother Cafe

208 Queen Street West
Toronto, ON M5V 1Z2
Canada
(416) 598-4719

Cuisine: Lao-Thai and pan-global

Chef Noy Phangnanouvong

The Queen Mum, as the restaurant is affectionately known by its many regulars, is housed in an historic building more than 150 years old in the heart of the Entertainment District.

Serves 6

2 tbsp vegetable oil

2 tbsp red curry paste

2 medium yellow onions, sliced

1 carrot, julienned

24 shrimp (16-20 size), peeled and deveined, tail on

1 red pepper, julienned

12 snow peas, julienned

1 large can coconut milk (18.6 oz/560 ml)

3 bunches glass noodles, soaked in cold water for 15 minutes, then drained

1 tbsp fish sauce

2 tbsp oyster sauce

3 lime leaves, julienned

Sprigs of cilantro for garnish

1. Heat oil in large sauté pan over medium high heat.

2. Add curry paste, onion and carrot and stir-fry until onion softens.

3. Add shrimp, red pepper and snow peas and stir-fry 2 minutes.

4. Add coconut milk and glass noodles and bring to a simmer.

5. Add fish sauce and oyster sauce; stir to combine.

6. Add lime leaves.

7. Serve immediately, garnished with cilantro.

Chef Noy Phangnanouvong

Phangnanouvong arrived in Canada in 1980 as a refugee from the war in Laos. She learned her cooking skills at home from her mother and aunts, joining The Queen Mum in 1989 as a prep person. She demonstrated her ease and talent in the kitchen, quickly picking up Western cooking methods and worked her way up to line cook, sous chef and, finally in 1995, to chef.

About Red Curry Paste

Different from spice powders, a paste is a combination of fresh herbs, roots, and other ingredients that are ground and mashed together with dry spices to form a paste. There are several kinds of curry pastes but the red used here, with its hints of ginger and garlic, is among the most popular. It has a little bite but is not too hot. Often, pastes are stir-fried in oil, because the oil reaches a higher temperature, allowing the paste to releases additional flavors from the spices and herbs that wouldn't come out with straight cooking.

POTATO SUJEBI IN SAKE CLAM BROTH

Little potato noodle rounds in a rich seafood broth

Serves 4

For the Sujebi Dough:

1 cup/200 g cooked, riced chilled potato

1½ cups/150 g all-purpose flour

1 tsp fine sea salt

1 tbsp cold water, or enough to form dough
    into logs

½ cup/120 g medium or large dried anchovies

1 large sheet of Kombu

3 dozen littleneck or 4 dozen Manilla clams

2 dried shiitake mushrooms (rehydrated in 1
    cup/240 ml hot water)

1 cup/240 ml dry sake

4 cups/950 ml cold water

Good quality sea salt

Fresh black pepper

1 small zucchini julienned

½ cup/30 g green onions,
    thinly sliced on the bias

½ cup/35 g toasted, shredded nori

1 tbsp toasted sesame seeds

Chef Kiyoung Sung

Kiyoung Sung is a graduate of the French Culinary Institute. He is currently a consulting chef at Saporis Engineering and is in the process of developing a food website called NYCutletiers.com.

1. Make sujebi dough by combining potato, flour and salt and water. Knead for about 5-7 minutes until uniform. Form into a long log about the size of a quarter in diameter. The dough should have a pliable consistency. Cover and refrigerate for at least 30 minutes.

2. Heat a large saucepan heat to medium, then dry-roast anchovies for 1-2 minutes.

3. Add kombu, clams, mushrooms, sake, and cold water and bring to a boil. Skim, then reduce to a simmer and cover.

4. Remove clams as they open. Separate the meat from shell and set aside.

5. Remove shiitake, slice caps very thinly, and set aside.

6. Strain broth through cheesecloth to remove any sediment.

7. In a large saucepan, bring strained clam broth to a boil and season with sea salt and black pepper.

8. Add zucchini.

9. Take sujebi dough out of refrigerator.

10. Holding dough with one hand start tearing tip end of dough using thumb and index finger of your other hand. You will want very thin rounds (about ¹⁄₁₆ inch/1-2 mm thickness) as dough will swell once cooked in broth. Using your thumb, roughly shape into rounds and place onto a nonstick silicone baking mat or lightly floured surface. Alternatively you can slice dough into rounds ¹⁄₁₆ inch/1-2 mm thick using using a very sharp paring knife. Then flatten against table surface with your thumb and roughly shape.

11. Drop the shaped sujebi dough pieces into broth and gently boil until cooked, about 3-5 minutes. A dozen pieces per serving should suffice.

12. Ladle evenly into warm bowls and top with clams, shiitakes, finely chopped green onions, shredded nori, and a sprinkle of toasted sesame seeds.

RED CURRY-COCONUT SOUP WITH GULF SHRIMP AND RICE NOODLES

Coconut milk gives a smooth and rich broth base to this shrimp and vegetable soup

Serves 4

2 tbsp olive oil

¼ cup/40 g red onion (small dice)

¼ cup/40 g celery (small dice)

¼ cup/40 g carrot (small dice)

¼ cup/45 g red pepper (small dice)

1 tbsp garlic, minced

3 tbsp ginger, finely minced

2 tbsp red curry paste

2 tbsp fish sauce

2 cups/475 ml clam juice

2 cups/475 ml chicken stock

4 cups/950 ml coconut milk

24 small whole shrimp (peeled & deveined)

8 oz/230 g rice noodles

4 tbsp cilantro, chopped

1 tbsp lime juice

1. Heat the olive oil in a saucepan to medium-high heat. Add the onion, celery, carrot, red pepper, garlic, and ginger and sauté for 5 minutes.

2. Add red curry paste and fish sauce. Then add clam juice and chicken stock. Lower heat and simmer for 15 minutes.

3. Add coconut milk and simmer for 3 minutes.

4. Add shrimp and simmer until the shrimp are cooked.

5. While the shrimp are cooking, place the noodles in a large bowl and add warm water to cover. The noodles will slowly hydrate and become flexible.

6. Once the noodles are soft, add to the soup along with the cilantro and lime juice.

33 Avenue B
New York, NY 10009
(212) 673-6903

Cuisine: Eclectic

Chefs Walter Hinds

Chef Walter Hinds

Hinds weaves many international flavors into the very varied menu at Poco Restaurant. The cultural inspiration for this dish is Vietnamese.

About Coconut Milk

Coconut milk is not the liquid found inside the coconut as many mistakenly think, but comes from pressing the fluid out of the thick white meat. A mainstay of many Asian dishes, like soups, curries, and sauces, it is high in several vitamins and minerals, particularly magnesium, which calms the nerves and helps maintain normal blood pressure.

SAIGON HOT AND SOUR SHRIMP SOUP

The tamarind base is what gives the "sour" to this hot and sour soup

Saigon Kitchen

526 West State Street
Ithaca, NY 14850
(607) 257-8881

Cuisine: Vietnamese

Chefs Bill Lam and Phuoc Tran

The Lam family opened the doors to Saigon Kitchen in 2011 to introduce authentic Vietnamese food to Ithaca, New York. With the belief that great food and cooking brings family, friends and loved ones together, the Lam family took a chance and opened what is now one of the hottest places to grab a bite in Ithaca—a restaurant that is home to foodies and adventurous diners.

Serves 2

½ tsp ground fresh garlic

1 tsp vegetable oil

3½ cups/820 ml chicken stock

½ cup/100 g sugar

½ tbsp sambal

½ stalk fresh lemongrass,
    bruised and chopped thin

1 tbsp tamarind base mix

5 oz/140 g large shrimp, cleaned and deveined

2½ tbsp fish sauce

¼ cup/40 g celery, sliced thin and diagonally

¼ cup/45 g pineapple

1 8oz/230 g package of vermicelli noodle

½ cup/50 g bean sprouts

1 ripe vine tomato, diced

Garnish:

1 tbsp sliced scallion head

1 tbsp cilantro

1 jalapeño, seeded and sliced thin (optional)

1. In a medium-sized pot, heat garlic in oil over low heat until fragrant.

2. Add chicken stock, sugar, sambal, lemongrass, and tamarind base and bring to a boil. Lower heat and simmer and for 10-15 minutes, stirring occasionally.

3. Add shrimp, fish sauce, celery, and pineapple. Cook until shrimp turns pink, approximately 2-3 minutes.

4. Add vermicelli noodles and cook for approximately one minute.

5. Divide bean sprouts and tomatoes into two soup bowls. Ladle the soup into the bowls and garnish with scallions, cilantro, and jalapeño. Serve immediately.

About Tamarind

Tamarind trees are common throughout Asia and in Mexico. The pulp from tamarind pods is sour and tangy, and is used as a base for hot and sour soup. It's a healthful fruit that's high in antioxidants and helps rid the body of "bad" LDL cholesterol. Tamarind is also a good source of potassium and iron.

SALMON SOBA A LA BT

A healthy dish full of vegetables and a variety of tastes and textures

BT

EAT LOCAL - THINK GLOBAL

BT

2507 South MacDill Avenue #B
Tampa, FL 33629
(813) 258-1916

Cuisine: French-Vietnamese

Chef BT Nguyen

BT is a gourmet restaurant with an international flavor, most notably its distinctive French-Vietnamese hybrid dishes.

Serve 2 for dinner; 4 for lunch

2 salmon steaks

1 tsp of organic miso paste

1 tsp roasted sesame seeds

1 tsp pure sesame oil

8 oz/230 g soba noodles

2 cups/175 g of baby bok choy

1 cup/60 g of sugar snap peas

½ cup/75 g of carrots, julienned

Fresh cilantro leaves, optional

Roasted sesame seeds, optional

For the Sauce:

2 tbsp olive oil

2 tsp sesame oil

2 cloves of minced garlic

2 tsp of minced ginger

2 scallions cut into 1 in/2.25 cm long pieces

2½ tbsp of mirin

3 tbsp of light soy sauce

2 tbsp of coconut water or coconut soda

½ tsp of palm sugar

Chef BT Nguyen

BT's obsession with the kitchen began as a child in Vietnam. At the fall of Saigon, a young BT began a long journey finally ending in the United States. After college, she pursued a career in the fashion industry. During that time, she continued her passion for cooking to the benefit of her friends. She finally started Exodus, a fashionable late-night café, in an unfashionable North Tampa location; everyone came. Ultimately, BT left the fashion industry to become a restaurateur.

BT has always been influenced by her appreciation for both traditional Vietnamese and classic French cuisine. Being in the restaurant industry for over 24 years, she took seminars with well-known chefs around the world, consulted for restaurateur Jean Denoyer at his renowned restaurant Le Colonial in San Francisco and in New York.

1. Rinse salmon steaks and wipe dry. Use tweezers to remove the pin bone. Then rub salmon with miso paste, sesame seeds, and sesame oil.

2. Cook the salmon steaks over medium heat, first with skin side down, until both sides are golden; the steaks will be medium rare.

3. Cook soba noodles according to package instructions. Drain and refresh under cold water. Set aside.

4. Blanch all vegetables in boiling water for 30 second. Drain and submerge under ice-cold water. Set aside.

5. Heat olive and sesame oils in a saucepan. Sauté garlic, ginger, and scallions for 30 seconds. Add the rest of the sauce ingredients and cook for another minute. Remove from heat.

6. Divide the noodles into 2 or 4 serving bowls, and place vegetables on top of noodles. Top off with salmon steak.

7. Pour the sauce over the salmon. Serve with fresh cilantro leaves and roasted sesame seeds, if desired.

SANUKI UDON

The stock for this udon noodle dish is soy based and flavored
with fish flakes—it is good hot or cold

Yoiya

1-28-1 Asakusabashi
Taito-ku, Tokyo 111-0053
Japan
81 3 3863 7723

Cuisine: Japanese

Chef Yoichi Okujima

Located in Asakusabashi, an old downtown
area of Tokyo, Yoiya specializes in Sanuki Udon,
which is a dish using the very popular wheat-
flour noodle that originated in the Sanuki district
of Japan. Yoiya offers an "izakaya" atmosphere
comparable to what would be a comfortable
neighborhood bar in the United States.

Serves 2

For the Stock:
1¼ cup/300 ml soy sauce
½ cup/100 ml sake
½ cup/100 ml sweet sake for cooking (mirin)
1 piece (4 x 4 in/10 x 10 cm) dried kombu
1 oz/35 g dried bonito flakes
1 oz/35 g dried mackerel flakes

½ lb/250 g sanuki udon noodle

Condiments:
¾ cup/50 g grated radish
¼ cup/20 g chopped green onion
2 tbsp roasted white sesame seeds
2 tsp grated ginger

1. Put all the stock ingredients in a pot and refrigerate overnight.

2. The next day, put the pot on the stove over high heat and turn off just before it comes to a boil.

3. Let sit for 5 minutes. Strain and allow to cool slightly.

4. Boil sanuki udon in a large stockpot for 15 minutes.

5. Rinse in cold water. Drain and put in a deep bowl.

6. Pour stock over udon.

7. Add condiments to taste.

Chef Yoichi Okujima

Hailing from the birthplace of sanuki udon, Chef Yoichi Okujima knew without question that he would make that dish the star of his restaurant and win over the prevailing Tokyoites' idea that "soba" noodles reigned supreme! He prides himself on bringing cultural diversity to his cuisine and offers dishes in his restaurant that reflect the changing seasons.

About Condiments

Condiments play an important role in seasoning Asian food. Many noodle dishes are served with a variety of condiments packed with strong flavors: spicy, sweet, bitter, salty. Diners custom-tailor the taste of their meal by adding the condiment combination that most appeals to them, allowing for a wide range of tastes for the same dish.

SEARED ATLANTIC SALMON WITH GREEN TEA SOBA NOODLES IN A GINGER LIME BROTH

This noodle soup is full of complex flavors from the zesty lime and hot pepper
to the green tea–infused soba noodles

Serves 4

4 tbsp thinly sliced green onions

3 tbsp finely chopped ginger

1 tsp crushed red pepper flakes

2 tbsp thinly sliced garlic

2 tbsp soy sauce (low sodium)

1 tbsp sesame oil

2 tbsp lime juice

¾ cup/180 ml clam juice

½ cup/120 ml chicken stock

4 6oz/170 g salmon fillets

Kosher salt

Black pepper

2 tbsp olive oil

12 oz/340 g green tea soba noodles, cooked

2 tbsp chopped cilantro

1. Heat a saucepan to medium high heat.
    Add green onions and ginger and sauté for
    three minutes.

2. Add red pepper flakes and garlic; cook for
    two more minutes.

3. Add soy sauce, sesame oil, lime juice, clam
    juice and the chicken stock. Simmer for
    five minutes.

4. Heat another sauté pan to medium high
    heat. Season the salmon to taste with salt
    & pepper. Add the olive oil to the sauté
    pan. Add the salmon and sear on one side
    for four minutes, then turn over and sear
    for an additional four minutes. (Serve
    medium rare.)

5. Heat the noodles in the broth, then divide
    the noodles and the broth among four
    bowls. Place a salmon fillet in each bowl.
    Sprinkle with the cilantro.

Poco

33 Avenue B
New York, NY 10009
(212) 673-6903

Cuisine: Eclectic

Chef Walter Hinds

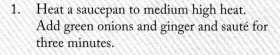

Chef Walter Hinds

Hinds weaves many international flavors into
the very varied menu at Poco Restaurant. The
cultural inspiration for this dish is Vietnamese.

About Sesame Oil

It's one of the good kinds! Sesame oil is chock full of anti-oxidants and high in mono- and polyunsaturated fats, which makes it helpful in reducing bad cholesterol. It comes in two varieties:

Light: Extracted from raw sesame seeds, it is pale yellow in color. A high smoke point means it's ideal for stir-frying and even deep-frying.

Dark: With a rich, nutty flavor, this dark brown oil is made from toasted sesame seeds. It's used primarily to add flavor and is often a key ingredient in marinades, dressings and sauces.

SESAME NOODLES WITH SHRIMP AND PEPPERS

Shrimp and peppers make this traditional peanut butter noodle dish
a more substantial main dish

Serves 6 to 8

1 lb/450 g vermicelli, thin spaghetti, or other
     long pasta shape

3 tbsp oil

4 cloves garlic, minced

30 large shrimp, shelled and deveined

2 medium bell peppers (1 red and 1 yellow), cut
     into strips

Salt and freshly ground pepper

For the Sauce:

4 tbsp oil

6 tbsp sesame oil

4 tbsp soy sauce

1 tsp salt

4 tbsp rice wine vinegar or white wine vinegar

4 tbsp smooth peanut butter

4 tsp grated fresh ginger

2 tbsp sesame seeds

4 tbsp chopped green onions, whites and tops

1. Cook pasta according to package
   directions, drain.

2. In a large bowl, combine oil, garlic, shrimp,
   and bell peppers; toss to coat. Season with
   salt and pepper.

3. Grill or broil until vegetables are slightly
   charred and shrimp are no longer
   translucent, about 3-5 minutes.

4. In a small bowl, whisk oil, sesame oil, soy
   sauce, salt, vinegar, peanut butter, and
   ginger until combined.

5. In a small dry skillet, toast sesame seeds
   over high heat, shaking the pan, until
   fragrant, about 2 minutes.

6. Pour sauce over noodles and toss to coat.
   Add shrimp and peppers to pasta.

7. Sprinkle with toasted sesame seeds and
   green onions. Serve warm or at room
   temperature.

National Pasta Association

750 National Press Building
529 14th Street, NW
Washington, DC 20045
(202) 591-2459

The National Pasta Association (NPA) is the trade association for
the United States pasta industry. The leading resource for all things
pasta, NPA was founded in 1904 and is comprised of manufacturing,
industry suppliers, and allied industry representatives. For more
information, recipes, or cooking tips, please visit www.pastafits.org.

About Sesame Seeds

Known to be the oldest oilseed crop (and also the one with the highest oil content), sesame seeds were domesticated over 3,000 years ago. When seed pods reach maturity they burst open with a pop—and some say this is where the expression "Open Sesame" comes from. With its nutty flavor and subtle crunch, adding sesame seeds to a dish enhances both the taste and the texture.

SHANGHAI LOBSTER NOODLES

Lobster tails, noodles and vegetables make this an elegant all-in-one-dish dinner

the
HURRICANE
STEAK & SUSHI

Hurricane Steak + Sushi

360 Park Avenue South
New York, NY 10010
(212) 951-7111

Cuisine: Steak and Sushi

Chef Craig Koketsu

Chef Craig Koketsu

Koketsu is the chef/partner of
Fourth Wall Restaurants in New
York City. The group is comprised
of upscale restaurants including
the flagship Smith & Wollensky,
Maloney & Porcelli, The Post
House, Quality Meats, Park
Avenue, The Hurricane Club, and
soon-to-open Berkeley.

From 1846-1873 this was the site of the famed "Hurricane Club,"
a tradition which began on the island of Lokoko in the South
Pacific Seas.

Captain Drake "Goldbelly" Stillman and his first mate, Delilah
"Little Rose" Netherlander, were aboard the legendary vessel *The
Junebug* when they were struck by a terrific storm. *The Junebug*,
transporting exotic foods from the region, 600-odd cases of
exquisite wines pilfered from the old French royal coffers, and an
undocumented cache of gold bullion, acquired, no doubt, through
dubious means, tumbled about the frothy sea, washed over by
waves three times the height of the ship's mast.

The Junebug met its end on a rocky promontory off the coast
of Lokoko. Goldbelly and Little Rose managed to get ashore,
clinging to the crates that carried their supplies. Subsequently,
they were captured and brought before the Royal Court of King
Pappu and Queen Ludellah to plead for their lives.

As the hurricane raged on, it was the foodstuffs and the rare
bottles of wine that not only saved their lives, but became the
basis for a wild and sumptuous feast. The King and Queen, in
turn, chartered the construction of a new vessel, named *The
Junebug II*, to assist their new friends in their journey homeward,
stuffing it to the brim with local delicacies.

Once returned to New York City, Goldbelly and Little Rose
began the tradition known as "The Hurricane Club," a yearly feast
for prominent merchants, diplomats, landed gentry, celebrated
artists, and high-ranking officers of the Navy—as well as a few
known pirates. In 1861, the King and Queen of Lokoko made the
long journey to dine with their dear friends, returning home laden
with the finest foods and drink from America.

The Hurricane Club funded several expeditions to the South
Pacific in search of gold bullion, which was never found.

Serves 6

4 Brazilian lobster tails

½ cup/120 ml olive oil

Salt to taste

1 tsp and 1 tbsp Korean chili flakes

¼ cup/40 g garlic, finely chopped

¾ cup/120 g onion, finely chopped

¼ cup/45 g jalapeño with seeds, finely chopped

4 in/10 cm piece of ginger, finely chopped

3 bunches hon shimeji mushrooms

8 hearts of palm, cut on a bias

½ cup/120 ml white wine

1 qt/950 ml whole canned tomatoes, pureed in a food processor

1 ¼ tsp sugar

½ head Napa cabbage, cut into half inch strips

1 package (24 oz/675 g) Shanghai noodles, cooked

1 bunch Thai basil chiffonade

Lemon juice to taste

1 bunch green onions, green part cut on a bias

1. Remove one of the lobster tails from the shell and cut in half. Marinate one half in ¼ cup/60 ml olive oil, a pinch of salt, and 1 tsp of Korean chili flakes for approximately 30 minutes. Roast the marinated half tail and the shell from the tail in a 350° F/180° C oven for 5-7 minutes, until cooked. Set aside and keep warm.

2. Remove the three remaining lobster tails from their shells; dice along with remaining half tail from above, and set aside.

3. Sweat the garlic, onion, jalapeño, and ginger until the onions become translucent, approximately 5 minutes.

4. Add 1 tbsp of Korean chili flakes, the mushrooms, and hearts of palm and cook until soft, approximately 5 minutes.

5. Add wine and cook until the liquid is reduced.

6. Add the tomato puree, then lower to a simmer. Add salt and sugar. Cook this mixture down until it becomes the texture of a tomato sauce. Transfer to a casserole dish and cool in the refrigerator.

7. To finish, heat up ¼ cup of olive oil and add the diced lobster, cooking for approximately 2-3 minutes. Add the tomato sauce to the pan and continue cooking for 5 minutes, then add the napa cabbage.

8. When everything is heated through, add the cooked noodles and chopped Thai basil. Adjust seasoning with salt, sugar, and lemon juice to taste.

9. Top with set-aside roasted lobster and chopped green onions. Stand the roasted tail shell in center of the dish for garnish.

SHRIMP-NOODLE SALAD

This colorful salad is delicious hot or cold

®

Cuisine: Modern American

Chef Michael Gilligan

Guests enjoy a menu that features deliciously composed small plates perfect for sharing; a wine list filled with unique varietals and specialty blends; an impressive raw bar boasting made-to-order fresh ceviches; and fresh-from-the-docks shellfish.

About Miso Paste

Miso is made by fermenting rice, barley, and/or soybeans with salt and a fungus. This traditional Japanese seasoning is a thick paste that is high in protein, vitamins, and minerals. The flavor of miso can vary widely depending on the ingredients used in the fermentation process. It can be salty or sweet, fruity or savory. It is widely used in sauces and spreads, for pickling meats and vegetables, and for soups.

Serves 2

3½ oz/100 g thin rice noodles

 Drizzle of sesame oil

7 oz/200 g snow peas or sugar snap peas

1 large sweet red pepper

1 large sweet yellow pepper

2 green onions

7 oz/200 g peeled, cooked shrimp (8-10 shrimp)

Handful of cilantro leaves

1 tbsp toasted black or white sesame seeds

For Thai Dressing:

1 shallot, peeled and finely chopped

4 garlic cloves, peeled and grated

2 small red chilies, seeded and minced

5 tbsp ginger, grated

½ cup/120 ml yuzu juice

1 cup/288 g miso paste

3 tbsp fish sauce

1 cup/240 ml light soy sauce

2 tbsp toasted sesame oil

3 cups/700 ml grape seed oil

Chef Michael Gilligan

Gilligan's diverse culinary adventures began immediately upon graduation from The College of Food and Arts in Birmingham, England, working as an apprentice chef at Michelin-starred restaurants in France and England, and at a number of top restaurants in New York City and Florida.

Put all the ingredients into a blender and add the oil slowly to emulsify.

1. Bring a kettle of water to a boil.

2. Place the rice noodles in a large heatproof bowl and pour boiling water over them, ensuring that the noodles are fully immersed. Cover the bowl with plastic wrap and let stand for 5 minutes, or until the noodles are tender but still retaining a bite. Drain and immediately toss with a drizzle of sesame oil to stop them from sticking together.

3. Blanch the snow peas in boiling water for 2 minutes until they are just tender, but still bright green. Refresh in a bowl of iced water, then drain well. Cut the snow peas on the diagonal into 2 or 3 pieces each.

4. Halve, core, and seed the peppers, then cut into long, thin slices. Trim and finely slice the green onions on the diagonal.

5. Put the shrimp, green onions, snow peas, and peppers into a large bowl and add the drained noodles, cilantro leaves, and sesame seeds. Pour the dressing over the salad and toss well to coat. Eat immediately, or chill until ready to serve.

SHRIMP YAKISOBA

A simple shrimp and noodle dish
easily adjusted for individual tastes

Serves 1

For Yakisoba Sauce:

1 cup/225ml oyster sauce

⅛ cup/25ml soy sauce

Salt

Pepper

Sesame oil, to taste

2 oz/60g of cabbage

1 oz/30g of onion

.5 oz/10g of carrot

1 oz/30g of green bell pepper

Vegetable oil

5 shrimp without the shell

3 oz/80g of bean sprouts

4 oz/113 g yakisoba noodles

Garnish:

Mayonnaise

Aonori

Grilled white sesame seeds

Beni shouga (Red pickled ginger)

1. Mix the ingredients for the yakisoba sauce and set aside.

2. Cut the cabbage, onion, carrot, and green bell pepper in bite-sized pieces.

3. Put a little vegetable oil in a pan and heat it up. When it's hot, add the shrimp, onion, carrot, and cabbage.

4. When the vegetables are cooked, add the bean sprouts and green bell pepper.

5. Boil the noodles. Then add them in the frying pan, mixing them with the vegetables.

6. Add sauce little by little, to your taste.

7. Put on a plate and garnish with mayonnaise, aonori, grilled sesame seeds, and red pickled ginger.

MADAKE イマダケ

Imadake

4006 Sainte-Catherine Street West
Westmount, QC H3Z 1P2
Canada
(514) 931-8833

Cuisine: Japanese

Chef Mineho Okunishi

Imadake strives to give everyone an authentic Japanese Izakaya experience. This extends to every aspect of the restaurant from the recipes and chefs to the sakes and the music. They believe that business should not come at the expense of the environment. All the ingredients are environmentally sustainable. The meats and vegetables are organic and the seafoods follow the "OceanWise" guidelines. Imadake recycles and uses energy-efficient appliances to lower the impact on nature.

Chef Mineho Okunishi

Chef Mineho Okunishi has worked in various restaurants in Japan over a period of ten years, and has experience in different kinds of cooking, from kaiseki to izakaya. His vision for Imadake's menu is being able to experience the taste of a real Japanese izakaya in Montreal without having to set foot in Japan.

SOBA NOODLES WITH CLAM SAUCE AND SEAWEED

With kelp and clams, this dish looks and tastes like it's straight from the sea

PALO ALTO GRILL
STEAKHOUSE
★ ★ ★ ★

Palo Alto Grill

140 University Avenue
Palo Alto, CA 94301
(650) 321-3514

Cuisine: eclectic

Chef Ryan Shelton

Palo Alto Grill serves locally sourced dishes with innovative twists, balancing top-selected meats with sustainably sourced fish and seasonal vegetarian cuisine, honoring the best of California cuisine: high quality and creative whimsy, translated into urban grill fare in a relaxed atmosphere.

Serves 6

2 cups/475ml dry sake

1 bulb garlic, sliced thin

½ cup/120 ml plus 1 tsp grapeseed oil

4 lb/2kg large clams, thoroughly washed and scrubbed

1 tsp red chili flakes

1 tsp cornstarch, dissolved in ⅛ cup/30ml water

1 package dry seaweed salad

1 tsp rice vinegar

1 gallon/3.8 L water, plus more as needed

4 tbsp salt, or to taste

6 bundles yakisoba noodles or fresh ramen

Juice of ½ lemon

Chef Ryan Shelton

Chef Ryan Shelton brings a rare combination of Michelin-star culinary establishment experience and a new kind of "open window" approach to menu development.

1. Bring sake to a boil over high heat in large sauté pan with lid.

2. Place garlic slices in a small saucepan and cover with ½ cup oil. Bring to a simmer over low heat, agitating occasionally until garlic turns uniformly gold. Be careful not to burn.

3. Once sake boils, add clams, cover and steam for 3-4 minutes until all clams open. Remove clams to a chilled bowl with a slotted spoon.

4. Continue to reduce sake and clam juice until only a cup remains.

5. By now, the garlic should be nicely gold; add the chili flakes and remove from heat.

6. Pick the meat from the clams and chop coarsely. When sake and clam juice are reduced, add the garlic, chili, and oil and bring to a boil.

7. Drizzle in the cornstarch slurry, whisking constantly. Remove sauce from heat and add chopped clams. Set aside.

8. Soak the seaweed salad in just enough water to cover.

9. After seaweed is restored, drain excess water and dress with 1 tsp grapeseed oil and rice vinegar. Reserve until time to serve.

10. When ready to serve, bring the gallon of water and salt to a boil in a large stockpot.

11. Simmer the noodles over high heat until tender, about 6 minutes.

12. Bring clam sauce back to a simmer. Add lemon juice.

13. Strain noodles and add directly to clam sauce.

14. Separate noodles and sauce into 6 bowls and top with seaweed salad; garnish with shells, if desired.

SPAGHETTI A LA DRUNK MAN

Looks can deceive; the sauce for this shrimp and pasta dish may look like its Italian cousin but has a distinctive Asian flavor

Ember Room

647 9th Avenue
New York, NY 10036
(212) 245-8880

Cuisine: Thai

Chef Ian Kittichai

Suspended above the entrance are four thousand authentic handmade Thai temple bells, whose soothing and resonant tones are said to create a peaceful and meditative state. Ember Room's menu takes on an existing culinary trend in Bangkok, described as "Thai comfort food." The menu is both firmly rooted in Thai tradition and seamlessly adapted to the selective integration of other culinary cultures.

Serves 2

1 tbsp vegetable oil

2 cloves garlic, finely minced

1 tsp crushed Thai chili

4 tiger prawns

2 tbsp diced bell peppers

2 tbsp diced onion

8 oz/230g spaghetti, cooked

2 tbsp chopped cherry tomatoes

1 tbsp oyster sauce

1 tbsp chili paste

2 tsp sugar

1 tbsp soy sauce

2 tbsp Thai basil

1. Heat oil in large frying pan or wok over high heat.

2. When the oil is hot, add garlic, crushed Thai chili, tiger prawns, bell peppers, and onions. Stir occasionally.

3. Add spaghetti and cherry tomatoes and stir for approximately one minute.

4. Mix oyster sauce, chili paste, sugar, and soy sauce together and then add to pan.

5. Stir for another 30 seconds. Stir in basil to finish.

Chef Ian Kittichai

Chef Ian Kittichai's path to culinary success started from very humble beginnings in Bangkok. Every morning he would rise at 3 a.m. to accompany his mother to the wet market to select the best meats, seafood, and vegetables for her neighborhood grocery. While Ian was at school, she would cook a dozen different types of curries. Upon his return home, Ian would push a cart through the neighborhood to sell his wares, shouting: "Khow Geang Ron Ron Ma Leaw Jaar!" (Hot curry coming!)

About Thai Chilies

Also known as Bird's Eye Chili, they've got some heat, measuring 50,000-100,000 Scoville Units (comparable to a lower-end habanero). They can be used both when green or after they fully ripen to red. With their super spicy yet fruity flavor, Thai chilies are favored for a variety of dishes such as salads and stews and sometimes are even eaten straight, as an accompaniment.

SPICY SEAFOOD SOBA NOODLE SOUP

Soba noodles in a spicy tomato broth with shrimp and squid

Skool

1725 Alameda St
San Francisco, CA 94103
(415) 255-8800

Cuisine: Japanese

Chef Toshihiro Nagano

The word "school" defines a social group of fish that swim in a coordinated manner to increase their families' overall defense, efficiency, and success. Skool thrives on the same principles and built their Skool in the same fashion--under the guidance of two husband-and-wife pairs, Toshihoro and Hiroko Nagano and Andy and Olia Mirabell.

Serves 4

For Tomato Compote:

5 tomatoes

¼ red onion, diced small

1 clove garlic

2 shiso leaves chiffonade

1 tbsp olive oil

1 tbsp salt

1 tbsp pepper

1 tbsp sugar

For Seaweed Compound Butter:

4 tbsp butter (room temperature)

⅛ tsp dried seaweed (grained)

For Lemon Grass Dashi Broth:

1 stick lemongrass

3 cups/700 ml water

1 sachet Dashi Pack

1 lb/400 g dried soba noodles

16-20 oz/450-560 g Monterey squid, cut in bite-sized pieces

16-20 black tiger shrimp

3 cups/700 ml dashi broth

1tbsp + 1tsp Thai red curry paste

4 tbsp Hon Tsuyu/soy sauce

12 tbsp parmesan cheese

1/2 bunch enoyki mushrooms, shredded

Shiso leaves chiffonade

1. Make tomato compote: Take the skins off the tomatoes by immersing in boiling water and then in ice water. Take the seeds out and cut into small dice. (*You substitute salsa without cilantro.) Add the red onion, garlic, and shiso. Coat with olive oil, salt, pepper, and sugar. Cover and let sit for 24 hours.

2. Make the seaweed compound butter: Have butter at room temperature until soft enough to whip. In a spice grinder, blend the dried seaweed until it is a powder consistency. Combine the butter and seaweed powder together.

3. Make the lemongrass dashi broth: Beat the lemongrass and put in a mid-sized saucepan. Add water and bring to a boil. Throw in a Dashi Pack and remove from the heat and let steep for 15-20 minute to fully extract dashi.

4. Cook the soba noodles as per the instructions on the package.

5. In a hot pan, cook the seafood together until fragrant. Add the dashi broth, seaweed butter, red curry paste, hon tsuyu, and reduce. Add the cooked soba and the parmesan cheese. Garnish with enyoki mushrooms, shiso, more salt, olive oil, and black pepper.

Chef Toshihiro Nagano

Chef Toshiro Nagano has spent his entire career learning and perfecting his trade in Japan, New Zealand, and California. Toshihiro was born and raised in Yokohama. He began working very young and became a chef at a traditional Japanese and sushi restaurant. In 1993, he relocated to California.

TEMPURA SOBA

Homemade noodles in a fish broth topped with fried shrimp and vegetables

Sarashinanosato — Chef Shigeyuki Akatsuka

3-3-9 Tsukiji
Chuo-ku, Tokyo
Japan
81 3 3541 7343

Cuisine: Japanese

Chef Shigeyuki Akatsuka

Since it opened in 1899, this soba restaurant has been popular for its handmade noodles.

While he was studying in college, Chef Akatsuka had already started to train himself by working at the honorable soba noodle restaurant Toranomon Sunaba, but he found it did not meet his needs. So he stayed back for one more year at college and took a traineeship at Nunotsume Sarashina, another place with a soba pedigree, where he learned how to make the best buckwheat soba noodles by hand—the basic principle in crafting good soba noodles. In his restaurant Akatsuka makes four different kinds of soba noodles. Since ingredients directly affect the quality of soba noodles, he pays utmost attention in selecting the buckwheat production area seasonally in Fukui, Ibaragi, Nagano, Fukushima, and Hokkaido in order to serve the best soba. "Persistence pays off" is Akatsuka's motto. He firmly believes that consistent efforts every day help one master the craft. He hopes people worldwide will become more familiar with the very rich, healthy, and nourishing soba noodle tradition in Japan's culture.

Serves 4

For Soba Soup:

3 oz/80 g dried bonito flakes

4 cups/900 ml water

¾ cup/180 ml soy sauce

1/8 cup/30 g coarse sugar

1 ½ oz/45 ml sweet sake for
cooking (mirin)

1 tsp sugar

1. Combine dried bonito flakes and water in a stockpot and boil for 60 minutes. This will be the soup base.
2. Add soy sauce, coarse sugar, mirin and sugar.
3. Boil the soup until the volume decreases by about 10%.
4. Remove from heat and refrigerate overnight.

For Tempura Fritters:

4 tiger prawns

Seasonal vegetables: 3 kinds of your choice, such as pumpkin, shishito pepper, eggplant, lotus root

Wheat flour

Eggs

Oil for frying

Garnish: radish, ginger, sliced green onions

1. Remove the prawn heads, peel off the shell, make cuts on the joints, and trim the tail.
2. Cut vegetables carefully so they can be evenly fried. Do not cut them too thick.
3. Dredge the prawns and vegetables in wheat flour. Then dip them in tempura mix which is made of equal amounts of wheat flour and beaten eggs. Fry them in oil.
4. Remove from pan and place on paper towels to drain off fat.
5. Divide noodles between serving bowls. Pour hot soba soup over top. Then add tempura prawns and vegetables.
6. Garnish with radish, ginger, and green onions.

How to Make Soba Noodles

For soba noodles (for 4 people):

1 ¾ cup/300 g buckwheat flour

½ cup/75 g wheat flour

½ egg

¾ cup/180 ml water

1. Knead buckwheat flour, wheat flour and egg in the water till it forms a dough.
2. Pat dough flat and slice into long, thin noodles.
3. Boil water in a large stewpot.
4. Put the sliced soba noodles softly in the hot water and boil them for 80 seconds. Don't overcrowd the water; do in batches.
5. Rinse the slimy soba in cold water twice, and then let drain in a colander.

THAI SHRIMP AND AVOCADO SOUP

This soup is bursting with the fresh flavors of cilantro, ginger and Thai spices

Serves 4

1 oz/28 g cellophane noodles, uncooked

1.5 lbs/700 g jumbo shrimp, shell on

2 tbsp peanut oil

5 cloves garlic, chopped

2 thin slices ginger

1 red onion, medium dice

1 tsp Chinese five-spice powder

6 cups/1.5 L chicken broth

¼ cup/60 ml shoyu (good quality soy sauce)

1 tbsp sugar

¼ tsp red pepper flakes (to taste)

½ cup/85 g very thinly sliced red or
    yellow bell pepper

2 large ripe avocados, diced

Seasonings: Chopped cilantro, thinly sliced green
onions, salt and pepper, fish sauce, lime wedges

Chef Kimberly Kulhanek

Kulhanek's mission as a chef is to bring the best in freshly prepared, local, health-supportive foods to the table, helping to create positive changes in dietary choices. While occasionally working in NYC restaurants and as a personal chef, Kulhanek created and executed her own culinary adventures. One of her favorites was a bimonthly "supper club" called Pig and Pepper that she ran for three years in Brooklyn and Queens, providing five- to six-course themed meals that catered to any individual special dietary needs and also had entertainment featuring local musicians and artists. Kulhanek attended Natural Gourmet Institute for Health and Culinary Arts in NYC.

1. Shell and devein the shrimp, keeping the shells.

2. Put 1 tbsp peanut oil in a large pot over medium heat.

3. Add shrimp shells, garlic, ginger, red onion, and five-spice powder. Cook for 2-3 minutes.

4. Add chicken broth, shoyu, sugar, and red pepper flakes. Bring to a boil, then reduce heat and simmer for 20 minutes. Let cool for 5 minutes, then strain out solids and return liquid to pot.

5. Pour boiling water over noodles to cover. Let sit for 15 minutes, then drain and set aside.

6. Heat 1 tbsp peanut oil in skillet and sauté the shrimp over medium-low heat for 3-4 minutes (until they are pink and start to curl). Remove from pan and set aside.

7. Add bell pepper and gently sauté for 1-2 minutes, just until hot through. Set aside with shrimp.

8. To assemble: Place noodles in a large serving bowl, top with shrimp and bell pepper. Add the diced avocado and sprinkle with cilantro and green onion.

9. Season the broth with salt and pepper and bring back to a simmer. Pour hot broth over the ingredients in the bowl. Add a splash of fish sauce and serve with a lime wedge. Enjoy!

TOYKO SEAFOOD RAMEN SOUP

Clams, scallops, shrimp and squid in a tasty ramen soup

Sushi Roku

8445 West Third Street
West Hollywood, CA 90048
(323) 655-6767

Other California locations in Santa Monica
and Pasadena, as well as restaurants in Los
Vegas, NV, and Scottsdale, AZ

Cuisine: Contemporary Sushi

Sushi Roku combines the finest, freshest fish from
pristine waters around the globe with the kind of artistry
that can only be provided by a mature sushi chef ensuring
superlative traditional sushi, together with a splash
of California innovation. Sushi Roku is a pioneer of
contemporary sushi, incorporating diverse, non-traditional
ingredients from Latin America (e.g., jalapeños) and
Europe (e.g., olive oil) into its edible works of art. This
unique culinary experience that bridges past and present
is the result of an eagerness to embrace new ideas and
a profound respect for tradition. Sushi Roku's bold and
diverse menu also offers an array of hot and cold specialty
appetizers and an extensive selection of exotic entrées.

Serves 1

1 tbsp olive oil

1 tsp julienned ginger

2 oz/60 g asari clams

1 oz/28 g shrimp, 26/30 size

1 oz/28 g bay scallops

1 oz/28g sliced baby squid

1 tsp oyster sauce

1 tsp soy sauce

Salt and pepper to taste

½ block ramen noodles

2 cups/475 ml ramen soup (recipe right)

6 sugar snap peas

1 tbsp chopped scallion

1 sheet dried nori

1. Heat olive oil and ginger in a large
   sauté pan.

2. Add seafood, oyster sauce, soy sauce, and
   salt and pepper.

3. Cook over medium-high heat until clams
   open, about 4-5 minutes.

4. Place ramen noodles in boiling water and
   boil for about 4 minutes.

5. Pour boiling ramen soup in serving bowl.
   Add ramen and sautéed seafood on top.

6. Garnish with warm snap peas, chopped
   scallion, and dried nori sheet.

For Ramen Soup:

½ cup/120 ml fish stock

1 ½ cups/350 ml bonito stock

1 oz/30 ml soy sauce

Combine all ingredients in a pot and bring to
a boil. This basic soup can be eaten plain with
noodles or it can be a base to which seafood,
meat, and vegetables can be added.

UNI SOMEN NOODLES

An elegant update to a simple Japanese comfort food: noodles,
in a creamy uni sauce with grated pecorino cheese and truffle finish

K-ZO

9240 Culver Boulevard
Culver City, CA 90232
(310) 202-8890

Cuisine: Japanese/sushi

Chef/Owner Keizo Ishiba

Keizo Ishiba's culinary repertoire
embraces novices and connoisseurs alike.
As a master of both Japanese and French
cuisines, Keizo embodies mature artistry
and commitment to traditions. His
award-winning sushi is at the heart of
his technique, but his vast menu of small
plate selections, rare sake options, and
spectacular desserts create an exquisitely
unique and varied dining experience.

Serves 2

1 oz/28 g shallots, finely chopped

½ cup/120 ml white wine

5 tbsp/70 g butter

6.5 oz/195 ml fresh cream

¼ cup/60 ml fish bouillon

3.2 oz/90 g sea urchin, chop half

Dash of soy sauce

Salt and pepper

1.8 oz/50 g somen noodles (2 bundles, dry)

Truffle, sliced

Pecorino cheese, grated

Pinch of chopped chives

A note from the chef

I invented this creamy dish as an unexpected addition to more traditional Japanese courses. With its rich sauce and fine ingredients, it quickly became a customer favorite. It also exemplifies two components of cooking that I am passionate about: using only the freshest ingredients and creating a beautiful presentation.

About Uni (Sea Urchin)

The creamy edible flesh of the sea urchin comes from the harvest of its sex organs, the gonads. This rich delicacy has long been thought to be an aphrodisiac.

1. Place the water in a medium sized pot to boil (to cook the noodles later).

2. In a separate skillet, bring the shallot and white wine to a boil and reduce the sauce to half its volume.

3. Add the butter to the skillet, gradually, stirring quickly to emulsify.

4. Add cream and boil the sauce down to thicken a bit more.

5. Add fish bouillon to the sauce and stir to thicken once again.

6. Stir in the chopped sea urchin, soy sauce, and salt and pepper to taste.

7. Place the somen noodles into the boiling water for just about 1½ minutes. Drain the water and wash the noodles with cold water. Drain again.

8. Add the noodles to the boiling sauce, tossing to coat the noodles completely.

9. Arrange the noodles on a plate and top with the remaining sea urchin and truffle. Sprinkle with pecorino cheese and chopped chives to finish.

VIETNAMESE CRAB NOODLE SOUP

Soup for a crowd with an abundance of flavors

butterfly
San Francisco - Embarcadero

Butterfly

Alcatraz Ferries, Pier 33
The Embarcadero
San Francisco, CA 94111
(415) 864-8999

Cuisine: Eclectic

Chef Rob Lam

The floor-to-ceiling windows at Butterfly offer dramatic views of San Francisco's bay. Robert Lam is committed to supporting San Francisco's diverse and innovative artistic communities. As part of his commitment, works by local artists adorn the walls of Butterfly.

Serves 24

For the Broth:

4 lb/2 kg shrimp shells

1 cup/240 ml shrimp paste

2 qt/2 l mirepoix

2 tbsp garlic and ginger, minced

6 stalks lemongrass hearts

1 cup/240 ml tomato paste

2 cups/475 ml red curry paste

2 tomatoes, rough chopped

1 bottle mirin

1 cup/240 ml fish sauce

4qt/4 l clam juice

2 qt/2 l chicken stock

1 bunch each cilantro and green onions

Lime Juice and Fish Sauce

½ lb/230 g galanga

12 kaffir leaves

1. Sauté shrimp shells, shrimp paste, mirepoix, garlic, ginger, lemongrass, tomato paste, and curry paste.

2. Deglaze with tomatoes, mirin, and fish sauce.

3. Add clam juice and chicken stock. Simmer until lemongrass, and mirepoix are soft.

4. Add cilantro, green onions, and chill. Adjust seasoning with fish sauce and lime. Run through a food mill, then strain and cool.

For the Raft:

14 whole eggs

2 lb/900 g crab meat, cleaned of shells

2 lb/900 g rock shrimp

1 tbsp each garlic and ginger, minced

½ tsp white pepper, ground

3 tbsp green onions, minced

2 tbsp tomato paste

2 tbsp shrimp paste

2 lb/900 g vermicelli

Garnish:

Red and green cabbage chiffonade

Red shiso leaf

Cilantro leaves

Green onions, chopped

Lime

1. Combine all ingredients in a bowl and whisk till thoroughly mixed.

2. Bring the broth to a gentle simmer and pour the raft into the broth. Make sure you scrape the bottom a couple of times to keep the eggs from sticking to the bottom of the pot. Otherwise do not touch the soup. Simmer gently until the egg is set. Turn off the heat and break up the raft.

3. Serve by pouring soup over just cooked vermicelli rice noodles.

4. Garnish with red and green cabbage chiffonade, red shiso leaf, cilantro leaves, and scallions. A squeeze of lime will also bring out flavor.

Chef Rob Lam

Robert Lam, named one of six "Rising Star Chefs" by the *San Francisco Chronicle*, was born in Vietnam and calls his cooking "Asian within Asian," pulling from culinary traditions from Vietnamese, Thai, Chinese, Japanese, and Korean. He is a graduate of the Culinary Institute of America.

YAKISOBA

A quick and easy shrimp and noodle dish that works for busy nights.

Serves 3-4

2 tbsp vegetable oil

1 package Yakisoba Noodles

½ cup/50 g bean sprouts

1 cup/340 g cabbage, chopped

½ cup/ 35 g shiitake mushrooms

¼ cup/ 18 g maitake mushrooms

½ lb/230 g shrimp, cleaned and deveined

2 tbsp yakisoba powder or tonkatsu sauce

1. Heat vegetable oil in a pan.

2. Add noodles and heat for 30 seconds. Pour ⅓ cup/80 ml of water into pan and loosen noodles in water. Cook until water evaporates.

3. Remove noodles from pan and set aside.

4. Add bean sprouts, cabbage, and shiitake and maitake mushrooms to the same pan and stir-fry for about 1 minute.

3. Stir shrimp into vegetable mixture and then add the noodles.

4. Lower heat and add in yakisoba seasoning or tonkatsu sauce to noodles and mix well.

Shibuya

4774 Park Granada
Calabasas, CA 91302
(818) 225-1560

Cuisine: Sushi

Chef Mark Shibuya

Named for a fashionable Tokyo neighborhood, Shibuya is a small sushi restaurant in Calabasas. The restaurant also features a small bar, and the atmosphere is quiet and relaxing.

About Bean Sprouts

The ubiquitous bean sprout, so often found in Asian dishes, is most commonly from the mung bean or the soy bean. Sprouts take typically only one week to be full grown and are more nutritious than the original bean that they come from.

YOSENABE

This dish allows you to take advantage of whatever seafood and vegetables are in season for the freshest possible flavors—different but delicious every time

檜

HINOKI
Japanese Restaurant • Sushi Bar

Hinoki

37 New Orleans Road
Hilton Head Island, SC 29928
(843) 785-9800

Cuisine: Japanese

Chef Teruyuki Suzuki

This authentic Japanese restaurant and sushi bar was opened on Hilton Head Island in 2001 by Hirofumi Ono and Teruyuki Suzuki.

Serves 2

For the Broth:

36 oz/1.5 L water

2 pieces of thick dried seaweed (kombu)
    3 x 3 in/7.5 x 7.5 cm

3 tsp soy sauce

¼ tsp salt

Slow boil all broth ingredients for 15 minutes.

Fish of your choice – such as:

cod, salmon, any white fish, scallops, crab legs,
    mussels, clams, whole shrimp

Vegetables:

4 scallion stems cut in half

3-4 sliced shiitake mushrooms

¼ pound of tofu cut in large cubes

Other vegetables to taste, such as spinach,
    Napa cabbage

8 oz/230 g shirataki noodles

1. Cook seafood and vegetables in kettle of
    hot broth for 5-6 minutes.

2. At the very end, add shirataki noodles
    and serve.

Chef Teruyuki Suzuki

Suzuki was manager and head chef at Kurama
Japanese Seafood and Steak House for more
than ten years before becoming co-owner,
manager, and chef at Hinoki.

About Kombu

Kombu is edible kelp or seaweed. It can
be bought fresh, dried, frozen, or pickled.
Widely available and very affordable, it figures
prominently in Japanese cooking. It is often used,
as here, in stocks and soups as a flavor enhancer.

MEAT

BEEF NOODLE SOUP

A quick and easy meal that makes good use of a small piece of steak

The Greedy Elephant

57 Queens Road
Weybridge KT13 9UQ
England
44 1932 856 779

Cuisine: Thai

Chef Arm Chaiyapruk

Thai food is all about contrasting and complementing tastes, such as hot, sour, sweet, and spicy, with every dish busting with flavor. At Greedy Elephant, every dish is prepared fresh to order, so whether you like your food mild or blow-your-brains-out hot, all dishes are prepared exactly as customers wish.

Serves 2

A handful of fresh rice noodles

3 cups/300 g bean sprouts

8 oz/230 g sliced sirloin steak

2 cups/475 ml water

1 cube beef bouillon or frozen beef stock

3 tsp fish sauce

2-3 tsp dark soy sauce

White pepper

A pinch of crushed coriander stems

1 garlic clove, chopped

Small handful of chopped coriander leaves

Green onions, chopped

1. Boil the noodles. Once they are cooked,
    strain and put into a bowl.

2. Add the bean sprouts to the boiling water
    and cook for about 30 seconds. Strain
    and add to the bowl with the noodles.

3. Boil the beef to desired doneness. Drain
    and add to the bowl with the noodles and
    bean sprouts.

4. Boil the water and add the beef bouillon.

5. Add the fish sauce, soy sauce, pepper, and
    coriander.

6. Return to a boil and pour the soup into
    the bowl with the other ingredients.

7. To finish, fry the chopped garlic in oil
    until golden and then add on top of your
    dish, along with the fresh coriander and
    green onions.

Chef Arm Chaiyapruk

Head chef Arm Chaiyapruk, who prepared
the savory magic in the picture on the facing
page, spent ten years running Kampan
restaurant in Southsea before bringing that
experience and flair to his new flagship
restaurant in Weybridge, Surrey.

About Fish Sauce

A staple in Thai and other Asian kitchens, fish
sauce is made from a concoction of fish and
salt that has usually been allowed to ferment
anywhere from a year to a year and a half. It is
often used to correct seasoning towards the end of
cooking or to add a saltier flavor to a dish. Often
you'll find fish sauce used in combination with
lime juice, which cuts the fishy smell and taste.

BEEF WITH BLACK BEAN SAUCE

A quick, clean-out-the-fridge meal for two

ChongQing

2808 Commercial Drive
Vancouver, B.C.
Canada V5N 4C6
(604) 254-7434

Two other locations,
one in Vancouver
and another in Burnaby

Cuisine: Szechuanese

Chef Paul Zhang

Chef Paul Zhang's pioneering ChongQing Restaurant has been Vancouver's go-to destination for hot and spicy Szechuan noodles for over two decades. His menu pays homage to the central Chinese city of ChonQing, known for its hot summers during which residents gorge on spicy food to induce sweating and lower body temperatures. Paul's signature specialty, Tan Tan Noodles, take their name from the carrying pole used by vendors who would roam the city offering the dish to sweltering citizens in need of a good lunch—and a good sweat.

Serves 2

1 lb/500 g cooked rice noodles

Soy sauce

Salt

8 oz/230 g sliced beef

Vegetables: sliced carrots, chopped white
    onions, sliced red and green bell peppers—
    any combination, as much as you like

½ tbsp garlic

1 tbsp black beans

1 tbsp light soy sauce

1 tbsp dark soy sauce

1 tsp sugar

1 tsp chicken bouillon

½ cup/120 ml chicken stock

2 tbsp cornstarch dissolved in a little water

1. Pan-fry warm rice noodles in a little
   canola oil with 1 tsp soy sauce and a dash
   of salt.

2. Pan-fry sliced beef and vegetables until
   beef is no longer pink and vegetables
   have softened a bit. Set aside.

3. In wok, heat a little canola oil and add
   minced garlic and black beans.

4. Add beef and vegetables to wok and
   mix well.

5. Add light and dark soy sauces, sugar,
   a dash of salt, chicken bouillon, and
   chicken stock, mixing well.

6. Slowly stir in cornstarch mixture and
   continue stirring until sauce thickens.

7. Ladle beef and vegetables over pan-fried
   rice noodles and enjoy.

Chef Paul Zhang

From an early age, Zhang knew the importance
of quality food. He is the third generation of
chef/restauranteurs in his family. Zhang has
expanded the family business to three successful
restaurants throughout Greater Vancouver.

About Soy Sauces

What's the difference between dark and light
soy sauce? Dark soy sauce contains molasses or
caramel (which gives it a darker color) and is
aged for a longer period of time than light soy
sauce. It is generally thicker and less salty. Light
soy sauce is saltier and lighter in color. It's the
kind that is most commonly used in cooking
and what you should choose if a recipe doesn't
specify light or dark. Dark soy sauce is mostly
used in marinades and sometimes in dipping
sauces. There are also mushroom- and shrimp-
flavored soy sauces.

BIRTHDAY CLAYPOT YEE MEIN

Yan Yat is the seventh day of the lunar new year, a day designated as "Everyone's birthday," and at this fun celebration, noodles are eaten to promote longevity—like this dish, which can be made with pork or chicken

Lily's Wai Sek Hong

www.lilyng2000.blogspot.com

Chef Lily Ng

Chef Lily Ng

Lily's Wai Sek Hong is a popular food blog administered by Lily Ng, a stay-at-home grandmother in Aurora, Colorado, who taught herself to cook and bake from cookbooks and by watching cooking programs on television.

About Oyster Sauce

This commonly used condiment in Asian cooking was created by a happy accident. In the late 1800s, a chef in the Guangdong province in China lost track of time while cooking his oysters one day. Noticing a strong smell, he looked in his pot—and instead of the usual clear liquid broth, he now had a thick, brown sauce, which proved to be a very popular addition to many foods. Other ingredients in oyster sauce are sugar and cornstarch, making it a sweet, viscous liquid that is often used in noodle stir-fries and to correct seasoning in other dishes.

Serves 4

Marinade for the meat:

2 tbsp light soy sauce

1 tsp tapioca starch

1 tsp sesame oil

Dash of pepper

1¼ lb/565 g pork or chicken slices

Oil for frying

4 pieces dried egg noodles (or Yee mein, if
    available) for 4 persons

2 tsp chopped garlic

4 cups/950 ml or more stock

4 tbsp oyster sauce

Salt and pepper to taste

2 tbsp Shaoxing wine

1 tbsp sesame oil

½ lb/230 g choy sum—washed and cut into
    1 in/2.5 cm lengths

2 tbsp tapioca starch mixed with 2 tbsp water
    for thickening

4 eggs

1. Mix marinade ingredients together and add pork or chicken. Let marinate in the refrigerator until ready to cook.

2. Heat enough oil for deep frying in a wok. When oil is 375°F/190°C, drop one piece of dried noodle in and deep fry until golden brown. Remove and plunge fried noodle into a large pot of cold water.

3. Repeat with the other 3 pieces of dried noodles. Discard oil and wipe wok clean. (If you have yee mein which are already fried, parboil and then put in cold water.)

4. Heat 4 tbsp oil in the wok and brown marinated meat slices.

5. Add in chopped garlic and sauté until fragrant.

6. Add in stock, oyster sauce, salt, and pepper, Shaoxing wine, and sesame oil and bring to a boil.

7. Add noodles and return to the boil. Reduce heat, cover wok and simmer until noodles are soft. (Add more stock if you want more sauce).

8. Add in choy sum and increase heat. Cook until choy sum is wilted but not mushy.

9. Thicken sauce with tapioca starch solution. Make sure the sauce is back to a boil and cooks for 1 minute before adjusting the taste with salt and pepper.

10. Divide boiling soup into four small clay or ceramic bowls. Immediately crack in an egg together with a dash of Shaoxing wine and sesame oil before serving. The egg will cook from the heat of the noodles.

BLACK PEPPERED BEEF UDON

Beef and noodles in a gingery sauce

Lily's Wai Sek Hong

www.lilyng2000.blogspot.com

Chef Lily Ng

Chef Lily Ng

Lily's Wai Sek Hong is a popular food blog administered by Lily Ng, a stay-at-home grandmother in Aurora, Colorado, who taught herself to cook and bake from cookbooks and by watching cooking programs on television.

About Chinese Celery

If a recipe calls for Chinese celery, substituting regular celery will not give a comparable result. Although they may look somewhat similar, Chinese celery has much thinner stalks, which are hollow, and can range in color from white to very dark green. It originally grew wild in Asia. It also has a much stronger flavor, and because of that it is not usually eaten raw but always cooked in soups or stir-fries.

Serves 3

For the Marinade:
½ tsp baking of soda
½ tsp sugar
1 tsp light soy sauce
1 tsp dark soy sauce
½ an egg white
1 tbsp oyster sauce
1 tbsp Shaoxing wine
1 tsp sesame oil
1 tbsp tapioca starch
2 tbsp water
2 tsp cooking oil

For the Gravy:
1½ tbsp freshly ground black pepper
3 tbsp oyster sauce
1 cup/240 ml chicken stock
1 tbsp cornstarch

½ lb/230 g beef filet/sirloin, thinly sliced across
    the grain
3 packets 7.20 oz/230 g Japanese-style udon
    noodles
Oil for frying beef and noodle
4-5 slices fresh ginger
½ cup/80 g Chinese celery, chopped

1. Mix together all marinade ingredients except the oil. Knead the mixture thoroughly into the sliced beef and when well mixed, add in the oil and knead again. Leave to marinate in the refrigerator for 30 minutes.

2. Mix gravy ingredients together and set aside.

3. Heat a pot of water to a boil, put in the udon, and turn off the heat. Let the udon sit in the hot water to keep warm.

4. Heat oil and when it is hot, fry the beef by batches until three-quarters cooked.

   Remove all but 2 tbsp oil.

5. Fry the ginger slices, then add in the warm udon and beef.

6. Stir-fry, then add in the gravy. Cook until gravy thickens. Add in celery. Serve hot.

BÚN THIT NUÓNG

Lemongrass Grilled Pork with Noodles

BellyLondon

E16 1EA London
United Kingdom

Cuisine: Canadian and Vietnamese

Chef Jane Tran

BellyLondon was founded in 2012 to bring Chef Jane's food to various festivals in London, such as Canada Day Festival, as well as to street food markets. BellyLondon offers catering, hosts supper club parties, and does private cooking workshops.

Serves 4

For Pork Marinade:

1 lb/450 g pork shoulder and ½ lb/230 g pork belly

3 lemongrass stalks, white and pale green parts finely minced

2 cloves garlic, minced

2 tbsp sugar

2 tbsp fish sauce

1 tbsp ground pepper

2 tsp sesame oil

2 tbsp dark soy sauce

1 tbsp oyster sauce

2 tbsp Shaoxing rice wine

For Scallion Oil:

¼ cup/60 ml of neutral oil, vegetable or canola

3-4 bunches of green onions, green part sliced thinly

Pinch of salt

For Dipping Sauce:

4 tbsp sugar

1 cup/240 ml hot water

4 tbsp fish sauce

¼ cup/60 ml vinegar

1 lime, juiced

3 garlic cloves, minced

Red chili, minced (optional, to taste)

1 1lb/400 g vermicelli, cooked al dente

1 cucumber, sliced

1 head of romaine lettuce, thinly chopped

Pickled carrots and daikon (optional)

Bean sprouts

Mint

Perilla

Lime wedges

Pork:

1. Combine pork and all marinade ingredients. Marinate for at least 1 hour or up to overnight.

2. Heat a griddle pan on high heat, grill pork. Set aside and let rest for 2 minutes, then slice.

Scallion Oil:

1. In a small pan heat oil on medium heat until warm (5 minutes).

2. Pour over sliced green onions. Season with salt and set aside.

Dipping Sauce:

1. Mix sugar with hot water until dissolved.

2. Add fish sauce, vinegar, lime juice, garlic and chili. Taste and adjust to your preferences.

Assembling the noodle bowl:

1. Divide noodles into six to eight bowls.

2. Top with grilled meat slices, cucumber, lettuce, pickled carrot/daikon, bean sprouts, mint, perilla, and lime wedges.

3. Put a spoonful of the scallion oil and 1-2 tbsps of dipping sauce over the noodles and serve immediately.

Chef Jane Tran

Tran is a globe-trotting Canadian-Vietnamese chef, inspired by everything from home-cooked local dishes from the streets of Asia to fine-dining restaurants in New York City. A graduate of the French Culinary Institute in NYC, Tran has worked alongside chefs such as Daniel Boulud, Michael Anthony, Anita Lo, and David Lee.

BÚN BÒ HUÉ

Spicy Beef Noodle Soup

BellyLondon

E16 1EA London
United Kingdom

Cuisine: Canadian and Vietnamese

Chef Jane Tran

BellyLondon was founded in 2012 to bring Chef Jane's food to various festivals in London, such as Canada Day Festival, as well as to street food markets. BellyLondon offers catering, hosts supper club parties, and does private cooking workshops.

Chef Jane Tran

Tran is a globe-trotting Canadian-Vietnamese chef, inspired by everything from home-cooked local dishes from the streets of Asia to fine-dining restaurants in New York City. A graduate of the French Culinary Institute in NYC, Tran has worked alongside chefs such as Daniel Boulud, Michael Anthony, Anita Lo, and David Lee.

Serves 8-10

For the Broth:

2 lb/900 g beef bones

2 lb/900 g pork bones

1 lb/450 g beef shank, boneless

1 lb/450 g ham hock, unsmoked

¼ cup/50 g yellow rock sugar or
    granulated sugar

1 tbsp salt

2 tbsp fine shrimp paste

8 -10 lemongrass stalks, bruised

1 large yellow onion

1 tbsp fish sauce

3 packages of Hue-style rice noodles
    (1.2 mm or larger, round rice
    noodles) prepared al dente

For Spice Mix:

¼ cup/60 ml neutral oil, vegetable or
    canola

4 tbsp annatto seeds

2 tbsp garlic, minced

2 tbsp shallot, minced

4-5 tbsp chili pepper flakes

1 tbsp paprika

1 tsp cayenne

Garnish:

1 large yellow onion, emincer (sliced
    paper thin)

3 limes, cut into wedges

2 cups/200 g bean sprouts

1 cup/32 g banana blossom leaf, shaved
    thinly (optional)

Rau ram

Perilla

1. De-gunking the bones: In a large stockpot, put beef and pork bones. Cover with water and lid. Bring to a rolling boil for 2-3 minutes, and then dump out bones into a large bowl or sink. Wash out pot and refill with water and return to stovetop. Meanwhile, give the bones a good rinse to remove scum and then return them to the pot.

2. To make the broth, first simmer bones and water for 1 hour, skimming the oil and scum intermittently.

3. Add in the beef shank, ham hock, sugar, salt, shrimp paste, lemongrass, onion, and fish sauce. Simmer for another 2-3 hours.

   Note: The ham hock will take less time to cook than the beef shank. Check on it after 1 hour. If the skin is tender, then it's done and you can remove it. Cover with some stock to prevent drying out, and set aside to cool. The beef shank will take longer to cook, about 2 hours. You can tell it is ready by feeling the tendon area of the meat; when the meat starts to fall apart under the pressure of your thumb or fork, it is ready. Remove, cover with stock, and set aside to cool. Slice ham hock and beef shank, once cooled, into thin slices. Do not slice while warm or the meat will shred.

4. Once the ham hock and beef have been removed, you can remove all of the bones, onion, and lemongrass. Or, you can opt to leave in the bones and simmer for an addition 2-4 hours on low, for additional flavor. Skim the broth again to remove any scum and then season with the spice mix below, as desired.

5. To make the spice mix, heat oil in a small frying pan on medium heat. Add annatto seeds and leave to infuse for 5 minutes. Strain and discard seeds. In the same pan, heat the annatto oil, garlic, shallot, chili pepper flakes, paprika, and cayenne. Sauté until fragrant. Remove from heat and add to broth by the spoonful, adjusting to your personal taste.

6. Assembling the noodle bowl: Warm up slices of ham hock and beef by simmering gently in some soup stock.

7. Fill bowls with noodles. Place generous amounts of ham hock and beef slices on top. Garnish with onion, lime wedge, bean sprouts, banana blossom, rau ram, and perilla.

8. Fill bowls with ladles of hot broth and serve immediately.

GANSO SOBA MESHI

Tasty yakisoba noodle dish with your choice of ground pork or chicken

Jidaiya Shun

4-15-1, Himonya
Meguro-ku, Tokyo
Japan
81 3 3713 2655

Cuisine: Japanese

Chef Amigo Hideki

The restaurant's main dish is Kyoto Kujo Negi, made with Kyoto kujo scallion, which Hideki has delivered fresh every day from Kyoto.

Chef Amigo Hideki

In 2002 Amigo Hideki moved from Kyoto to Tokyo with the goal of making the Kyoto Kujo Negi the best scallion in Tokyo and to run a restaurant that, like the scallion, would grow in reputation. He continues to run the restaurant today with the same passion.

Serves 4

4 tsp oil

14oz/400g of finely chopped raw pork or chicken

2 cloves of garlic, minced

2 packs of Yakisoba noodle, cooked

2 bowls of steamed rice, cold is better (about 2½ cups/400g)

1½ oz/40g of minced red pickled ginger

1 tbsp/15 ml oyster sauce

1 tsp of soy sauce

2 tsp Worcestershire sauce

1 tsp of garam masala

1. Heat 2 tsp oil in a wok or heavy skillet over high heat. Add pork or chicken with minced garlic. Add salt and pepper to taste. Stir-fry until meat is cooked, about 7 minutes. Set aside.

2. Wipe out pan and heat remaining 2 tsp oil over high heat. Add boiled noodles and cold steamed rice. Stir and chop finely until dried out.

3. Mix meat and noodle/rice mixture together and stir in ginger.

4. Add oyster sauce, soy sauce, Worcestershire sauce, and garam masala and stir well.

5. Serve with a sunny-side up egg on top, if desired.

INDOCHINE HERB-TOSSED NOODLES WITH GARLIC PEPPER PORK

A warm Asian salad topped with grilled pork

Banana Tree

103 Wardour Street
W1F 0UQ London
England
44 20 7437 1351

Multiple locations in London

Cuisine: Indochinese

Chef William Chow

Banana Tree showcases the best dishes from various Southern Asian countries, including Vietnam, Laos, Cambodia, Thailand, Malaysia, and Singapore.

Chef William Chow

Chow opened his first Banana Tree cafe in 1991 and now has six restaurants in London with a special interest in providing great healthy food from a variety of Asian cuisines. His restaurants now also serve as an "in-house" chef training academy.

Sweet and Sour Dressing

¼ cup/50 g brown sugar

¼ cup/50 ml Asian fish sauce

¼ cup/50 ml vinegar

1/8 cup/25 ml lime juice

½ cup/100 ml water

Finely chopped crushed garlic, to taste

Finely chopped red chilli to taste

Mix dressing ingredients together and stir until sugar dissolves completely. Set aside.

Serves 4

12 oz/300g rice vermicelli
 (Most other oriental noodles will also work well.)

For Grilled Garlic Pepper Pork:
1 ½ lb/600 g pork shoulder steaks (½ in/1.25 cm thick)
1/8 cup/20 ml fish sauce
1/8 cup/20 ml oyster sauce
2 ½ tbsp palm sugar (or substitute with dark brown sugar)
1 tbsp corn flour
8 turns black pepper
3 cloves garlic, peeled, crushed flat and roughly chopped
3 tbsp vegetable oil for marinating

Accompaniments:
2 cups/200 g bean sprouts (washed and drained)
2 cups/200 g batavia lettuce (roughly chopped)
40 mint leaves
20 rau ram mint leaves
20 sweet basil leaves
4 heads of sawtooth herb (roughly chopped)

Garnish:
4 tbsp crushed peanuts
4 tbsp crispy fried shallots
 (available from most Asian food shops)

1. Cook noodles in plenty of boiling water till soft. Drain properly and spread flat. Cool to room temperature.

2. Mix all Grilled Garlic and Pepper Pork ingredients together and allow to marinate for at least 30 minutes.

3. Pan-fry the steaks with a little oil in a hot frying pan (preferable nonstick) over medium heat for approximately 2 minutes on each side or until fully cooked. You may have to do them in batches.

4. To assemble: Place the noodles, accompaniments, and the cooked meat in a deep bowl.

5. Garnish generously with the peanuts and crispy shallots. Serve the dressing separately so that your guests can pour on the amount they wish. Mix well.

KHANOM JEEN NAM NGIAW

A noodle dish richly infused with flavor by using several types of pork

ชักว่าว Chạk ẁāw

Verb. Thai: ชักว่าว, Chạk ẁāw 1. To fly a kite.

Chak Wow

214 Rue Beaubien East
H2S 1R4
Montreal, Quebec, Canada
(438) 862-6134

Cuisine: Thai

Chef Jesse Mulder

Chak Wow is a Thai delivery service that caters to the Little Italy and Mile End areas of Montreal.

About Dok Ngiaw

These flowers from the red cotton tree are harvested when they blossom in the winter, usually December to February. The flowers are dried before they are packaged and must soaked in warm water for about 30 minutes before they can be added to a dish. Their flavor is subtle, but key to this classic pork noodle dish. There are no substitutions but luckily they can usually be found in Asian grocery stores.

Chef Jesse Mulder

Jesse Mulder was traveling to Thailand en route to Australia when he fell in love with the country and its food. After traveling back and forth, he moved to Thailand for four years, where he lived with a Thai family in Bangkok and learned to cook. Even after a range of cooking courses, Muller learned to cook from various sidewalk chefs and his Thai "mother." The base for the recipe included here is from a friend, Takkinai Rutanopope, from the Chiang Mai province. Mulder suggests that the ingredient quantities for this recipe be used as a guideline only, and each chef should tweak them as desired to suit his or her own taste.

Serves 4

1 lb/450g pork spareribs, cut into 1 inch lengths

1½ qt/1.5 L stock or water

Pinch of salt

18 oz/500 g khanom jeen noodles or equivalent

¼ cup/60 ml cooking oil or rendered pork fat

¼ cup/50 ml light soy sauce

1 tbsp palm sugar

½ lb/250 g fatty minced pork

2¼ lb/1 kilo coarsely chopped tomatoes or cherry tomatoes

30-40 dok ngiaw (dried flowers of the red cotton tree), soaked in lukewarm water for 30 minutes or until pliable but not soft, and then drained

4 tbsp tao jeow (fermented soybean paste)

8 pork blood cakes, cut into 1 inch cubes

For the Paste:

Pinch of salt

8 cloves garlic, halved

4 long red chili peppers

10 dried birds-eye chili peppers

2 red shallots, chopped

3 tbsp red turmeric, chopped

1 tbsp galangal, chopped

3 coriander roots

1½ tbsp Thai shrimp paste

Garnish:

Deep fried garlic

Coriander leaf

Chopped spring onion

Chopped red shallot

Chopped rinsed pickled mustard greens

1. Place the spareribs, stock or water, and salt in a large pot and bring to a boil, then reduce to a low simmer and let cook, stirring occasionally and skimming off the foam.

2. Boil noodles until cooked soft, not al dente. Rinse in cold water. Drain and set aside.

3. Meanwhile, using a granite mortar and pestle, pound together your chili paste by adding all the paste ingredients one by one and pounding until the paste is smooth.

4. In a wok or large pan, heat the oil or rendered fat and fry the chili paste until fragrant, stirring continuously.

5. Season with soy sauce and palm sugar.

6. Add the minced pork and continue frying, stirring pork around to break it up into small pieces.

7. Add tomatoes and simmer for about 5 minutes, then pour the whole lot into the pot with the spareribs.

8. Add dok ngiaw flowers along with tao jeow and pork blood cakes and continue simmering until flowers are soft, about another 7-10 minutes.

9. Check your seasoning and adjust if need be: the taste should be rich and meaty, salty and not too spicy, and a bit sour from the acidity of the tomatoes.

10. Serve your nam ngiaw with the noodles and garnish with deep fried garlic, coriander leaf, chopped spring onion, chopped red shallot, and pickled mustard greens. Other garnishes include deep-fried pork skin, chopped snake beans, and deep-fried dried chilies.

KUAY TIAW MU TUN

Pork Rib Noodle Soup

ISSAYA
SIAMESE CLUB

Issaya Siamese Club

Thanon Chuea Phloeng, Thung Maha Mek, Sathon, Bangkok 10120, Thailand
66 2 672 9040

Cuisine: Thai

Chef Ian Kittichai

The menu at Issaya features Chef Ian's unique signature Thai cuisine using traditional ingredients and flavors with international and progressive cooking methods. The restaurant features an ever-changing market menu that highlights seasonal specials direct from the market. Issaya also features the Chef's garden where guests can see aromatic Thai herbs grown year-round. Chef Ian is a pioneer in farm-to-table dining in Thailand and aims to incorporate his beliefs regarding the purity and freshness of ingredients into Issaya.

Serves 4

For Pork ribs:

14 oz/400 g lemongrass, whole stalks

4 galangal

Small handful kaffir lime leaves

12 oz/350 g pork ribs

1 qt/1 L water

1. Place all ingredients into a pot and bring to a boil. Let simmer for 4 hours or until ribs are tender.

2. Take ribs out of liquid to cool, then cut into 4 pieces and broil with Kraduk Mu Ob Sauce (below) for 5 to 8 minutes.

For Kraduk Mu Ob Sauce:

2½ cups/500 g palm sugar

6 oz/160 g salted yellow bean paste

9oz/250 g nam phrik kaeng daeng (red curry paste)

In a saucepan, melt palm sugar on low heat. Add bean paste and red curry paste, stir until well combined.

Chef Ian Kittichai

Chef Ian Kittichai's path to culinary success started from very humble beginnings in Bangkok. Every morning he would rise at 3 a.m. to accompany his mother to the wet market to select the best meats, seafood, and vegetables for her neighborhood grocery. While Ian was at school, she would cook a dozen different types of curries. Upon his return home, Ian would push a cart through the neighborhood to sell his wares, shouting: "Khow Geang Ron Ron Ma Leaw Jaar!" (Hot curry coming!)

For the Soup:

1 qt/1 L pork or chicken stock

3 cinnamon sticks

2 star anise

1 tbsp coriander roots

1 tbsp garlic

1 tbsp black peppercorn

2 tsp sweet dark soy sauce

3 tbsp soy sauce

1. Put all ingredients into a pot, bring to a boil, and let simmer for 30 minutes.

2. Strain through a fine-meshed sieve and discard solids.

12 oz/320 g thin rice noodles

½ cup/40 g bean sprouts

1 tsp vegetable oil

1 qt/1 L soup

3 tbsp chopped spring onions

1. To assemble: Blanch noodles and bean sprouts in boiling water. After draining, toss with vegetable oil and place into serving bowls.

2. Put pork ribs on top of the noodles.

3. Pour soup over the ribs.

4. Garnish with spring onion.

5. Serve immediately.

MALAYSIAN LASAGNA

Homemade "lasagna" noodles and alternating layers of beef and crunchy salad fillings

Hawaii Food Tours
www.HawaiiFoodTours.com
Chef Matthew Gray

Chef Matthew Gray

Gray, a former professional chef, has cooked for movie stars and rock and roll bands. He was the food writer and restaurant critic for Hawaii's largest newspaper for several years before starting Hawaii Food Tours, voted the best tour in Hawaii for the past two years.

Serves 8-10

For Rice Noodles:

You will need a steamer to make these.

¾ cup/115 g rice flour

1 tbsp tapioca flour

1 tbsp cornstarch

¼ tsp salt

1 tbsp oil

¾ cup/180 ml cold water

½ cup/120 ml boiling water

* You may wish to add some thinly sliced green onion to batter.

1. Spray two 8-in/20-cm pie pans with vegetable oil. Bring steamer to a rolling boil.

2. In a medium bowl, combine the rice flour, tapioca flour, cornstarch, salt and oil.

3. Add cold water and stir until smooth. Stir in the boiling water and chopped green onion.

4. Reduce the heat for the steamer so that the water is barely bubbling.

5. Give the batter a quick stir, then ladle ¼ cup/60 ml of the batter into a pie pan tilting the pan to spread the batter evenly.

6. Cover and steam for about 5-6 minutes, or until the sheet has cooked through.

7. Place the hot pan into a dish of cold water for a few minutes to cool down, or place on a rack in front of a blowing fan for several minutes.

8. Use a flat spatula to loosen the sheet along one edge, then roll it up loosely. Transfer to a plate.

9. Repeat with the remaining batter and pie tins, cleaning and oiling the pans each time, and replenishing the simmering water in steamer as necessary.

10. Noodles are now ready to be used in the lasagna.

For Malyasian Coconut Crunch Salad Layer:

For Malyasian Coconut Crunch Salad:

1 cup/150 g jicama, thinly sliced

1 red onion, thinly sliced

1 carrot, peeled and grated

1 red bell pepper, seeded and thinly sliced

3 cups/300 g bean sprouts

1-2 hot red chiles, seeded and finely chopped

1 small handful mint leaves, roughly chopped

1 small handful cilantro, roughly chopped

½ cup/40 g shredded coconut

For the Dressing:

8 tbsp fish sauce

4 fresh limes, juiced

4-6 tsp coconut palm sugar

2 in/5 cm length of ginger, peeled and grated

1. Put all salad ingredients except coconut in a glass dish or bowl.

2. Make the dressing: whisk the fish sauce, lime juice and sugar together in a large bowl. Add the grated ginger and mix well.

3. Pour dressing over salad, making sure that ingredients are submerged in the dressing. Refrigerate and allow salad to macerate for 2-24 hours.

4. Toast the coconut in a small pan over low-medium heat, stirring continuously, until the coconut becomes fragrant and turns golden brown. Transfer to a flat plate to cool, and set aside.

4. When ready to assemble the lasagna, sprinkle the toasted coconut over the salad and mix well.

For Beef Rendang Layer:

Spice Paste:

5 shallots, peeled and cut in half

1-2 in/2.5-5 cm piece of galangal (or ½ tsp galangal powder)

3 lemongrass stalks (white part only)

4 cloves garlic

¼ cup/20 g toasted coconut

1 in/2.5 cm piece of ginger

10 peppercorns (black or red)

8 dried chilies (not chipotle), soaked in warm water and seeded

6 tbsp canola or peanut oil

1 cinnamon stick

4 cardamom pods

3 star anise

2 cloves

2 lb/900 g boneless beef short ribs (cut into cubes)

2 lemongrass stalks, white part only (crushed with tenderizing mallet)

1 can thick coconut milk

1½ cups/350 ml water

2 tsp tamarind paste

6-8 kaffir lime leaves, very finely sliced

2 tbsp sugar (or palm sugar), or to taste

Salt, to taste

1. Chop all spice paste ingredients and then blend in a food processor until fine.

2. Heat the oil in a stew pot, add the spice paste, cinnamon, cardamom, star anise, and cloves, then stir-fry over medium heat until aromatic.

3. Add the beef and the pounded lemongrass and stir slowly for 1 minute.

4. Add the coconut milk, water, and tamarind paste, then simmer over medium heat, stirring frequently until the meat is almost cooked.

5. Add the kaffir lime leaves and sugar, stirring to blend well with the meat.

6. Turn heat to low, cover and simmer for 60-90 minutes, or until the meat is soft and tender, and the gravy has dried up.

7. Add salt to taste. Then, if not sweet enough, add more sugar.

To assemble: Place one lasagna noodle in a deep, round metal or ceramic dish. Add a layer of beef rending, then another noodle. Continue alternating noodles and fillings, using Coconut Crunch Salad for every second or third layer, until fillings and noodles are all used. Serve immediately.

MEE HUN BA CHANG PHUKET

Wok fried rice noodles with egg, chives, and bean sprouts,
served with clear pork sparerib soup

MUI NE
RESORT & SPA

La Sala Restaurant

888 Moo3, Tumbon Mai Khao,
Amphur Thalang, Phuket 83110
Thailand
66 76 336 100

Cuisine: Thai

Chef Poonsak Saovamol

Featuring a contemporary Thai
design, La Sala presents both
traditional and Southern Thai
Cuisine in a charming lagoon-
side setting.

Serves 2

For Wok Fried Rice Noodles:

⅓ lb/150 g rice noodles

1 tsp sweet black soy sauce

Cooking oil

1 tbsp chives

¼ cup/20 g bean sprouts

1 long red chili, sliced

1 ½ tbsp chicken stock

1 Thai omelet. shredded, (recipe below)

2 tsp soy sauce

2 tsp oyster sauce

2½ tsp white sugar

Garnish:

1 crispy Thai omelet (recipe below)

¼ cup/20 g bean sprouts

1 tbsp chives

Lime wedges

Condiments:

Roasted peanuts, crushed

Chili powder

Fried shallots

Fried garlic

White sugar

For Pork Sparerib Soup:

1 ½ cups/300 ml pork stock

1 (2 oz/50 g) young pork sparerib

1 clove garlic, peeled

¼ oz/5 g resh galangal

¼ oz/5 g coriander root

2 tsp black pepper

1 oz/30 g shiitake mushrooms

¼ oz/5 g kaokee (goji berry)

Seasonings:

2 tsp soy sauce

2 tsp seasoning soy sauce

2 tsp fish sauce

Garnish:

2 tsp green onion

For the Noodles:

1. Soak the noodles in water for about 5 minutes.

2 . Then put them in a bowl and mix together with black soy sauce until noodles are brown.

3. Heat the oil in a wok. Add the noodles and all remaining ingredients (except garnish and condiments) and stir-fry until all ingredients are mixed together and heated through.

5. Plate the noodles and put garnish on the top.

6. Serve condiments on the side.

For the Soup:

1. Place all the soup ingredients (except for seasonings) in a stockpot and bring to a boil.

2. Continue boiling until the pork sparerib is soft.

3. Mix the seasonings together and add to soup.

4. Pour soup into two bowls and garnish with green onions.

To make Thai Omelet:

1. Heat ¾ cup/200 ml oil in a frying pan.

2. Whisk one egg and then pour into hot cooking oil.

3. Fry in a round pancake shape.

4. Once cooked, remove and roll like a cigar, then shred finely with a knife.

To Make Crispy Thai Omelet:

1. Heat ¾ cup/200 ml oil in a frying pan.

2. Whisk one egg. Then, dip your fingers into the egg and wave hand over the pan of hot oil.

3. Cook egg strips until cripsy.

4. Continue until all egg is used.

PAD SEW EAW

Pork, broccoli, and scrambled egg with noodles and a sweet sauce

Khao San Road

326 Adelaide Street West
Toronto ON M5V 1R3
Canada
(647) 352-5773

Cuisine: Thai

Chef Chantana "Top" Chapman

Khao San Road is a massively popular casual restaurant serving Thai food in the heart of Toronto. It has an abundance of appreciative fans. From the start, its approach has been simple: a short menu, affordable prices, and a happy team with no attitude.

Serves 2

1 cup/200 g Chinese broccoli (Gai lan)

2 cloves garlic, minced

½ lb/250 g pork, sliced

1 tsp seasoning soy sauce

1 egg

1 lb/450 g wide rice noodles

1 tbsp sweet soy sauce

2 tbsp oyster sauce

1. Wash Chinese broccoli, discard yellow or hard leaves, and peel stems' skin. Cut leaves into 2-in/5-cm lengths, and slice peeled stems.

2. Heat oil in a wok on medium heat. When oil is hot, add minced garlic and fry until fragrant.

3. Add pork, stir until the pork is partially cooked, then add seasoning soy sauce.

3. Stir-fry until the pork is completely cooked. Make room for egg in the middle. Crack the egg, then scramble it with a spatula and spread in a thin layer.

4. When the egg is cooked, cover with the pork and stir-fry thoroughly. Add wide rice noodles with sweet soy sauce and stir well.

5. Add Chinese broccoli and oyster sauce. Stir to mix all together, then remove from heat.

6. Serve immediately.

Chef Chantana "Top" Chapman

Growing up in Bangkok, Thailand, Chef Chantana "Top" Chapman's mother taught her to appreciate and love food from a young age. Later she would study culinary arts in her home city, before coming to Canada in 2008. As a certified Thai Chef, she brings vast knowledge and skills ranging across the culinary landscape of Thailand with a focus on Bangkok and central style street food to Khao San Road.

Some of Chef Top's other passions include dancing; the love of her community, both Toronto and Thailand; animal welfare, particularly the majestic elephants of Thailand; and, of course, her daughter.

About Chinese Broccoli

It's almost the opposite of regular broccoli: Instead of large florets and small side leaves, Chinese broccoli is a leafy vegetable with a few very small florets. The taste is similar but the Chinese broccoli has a stronger, slightly more bitter flavor. Broccolini is a hybrid of Chinese broccoli and broccoli.

PAD THAI WITH SHRIMP OR MEAT

This free form recipe lends itself to experimentation: Add amounts according to your palate and the number of people you're serving—the taste should be sweet and sour and not too salty

Thai Thai Cafe

13605 Roscoe Boulevard
Panorama City, CA 91402
(818) 786-2233

Cuisine: Thai

Chef Niasporn Komolha

Chef Nisaporn Komolha

Niasporn grew up in Thailand and wanted to bring healthy and delicious Thai cuisine to America. After selling her food at farmer's markets across Los Angeles and being a private chef, she decided it was time to open Thai Thai Cafe.

Shrimp, pork, chicken or beef

Eggs

Oil

Green onion stem

Fermented chopped dry Chinese radish

Soy bean curd (Tofu)

Pad Thai noodles

Chicken broth

Tamarind sauce

Sugar

Fish sauce

Bean sprouts

Ground peanuts

Lime wedges or orange slices

1. Stir-fry shrimp (or meat) and eggs together in a little oil until eggs are cooked over easy. Remove from the pan and set on a plate to drain out the grease.

2. Stir-fry green onion stem, radish, and tofu.

3. Add pad thai noodles and some chicken broth and cook until noodles begin to get soft.

4. Then add shrimp and eggs that were prepared earlier.

5. Stir in tamarind sauce, sugar, and fish sauce until you see that the noodles are cooked.

6. Add bean sprouts and quickly stir for a few seconds.

7. Plate the noodles. Sprinkle with ground peanuts and serve with a piece of lime or orange.

About Chinese Radish

Also known as daikon, a Chinese radish may
have a similar sharp bite to a traditional radish
but looks more like a fat, white carrot. In fact,
daikon literally translated is long (dai) root
(kon). For this recipe, the radish is dried and
fermented, giving it a saltier, pickled flavor.

PORK YUZU SPAGHETTI

Pungent yuzu pepper paste gives this spaghetti dish some kick

Serves 2

12 oz /320 g spaghetti

1 oz/30 g Yuzu pepper paste

2 tbsp unsalted butter, softened

⅓ lb /150 g pork loin, thinly sliced

5 green onions, green stalk part only

2 tbsp soy sauce

⅓ cup/60 g yellow onions, slightly sautéed

1¼ cups/300 ml dashi soup

1. Cook spaghetti in boiling water until al dente.

2. While spaghetti cooks, mix yuzu pepper paste and butter together.

3. Sauté pork on both sides until brown.

4. Cut the stalks of 2 green onions into 1" pieces and add to pork.

5. Add soy sauce, yellow onions, and dashi soup.

6. Stir in yuzu/butter mixture and mix well.

7. Reduce sauce until desired consistency.

9. Add cooked spaghetti and toss with sauce.

10. Garnish with the rest of green onion stalks, thinly sliced

Bloom Restaurant

24503 Narbonne Avenue
Lomita, CA 90717
(310) 325-5000

Cuisine: Japanese-style Italian

Chef Miko Matsumaru

Bloom serves Japanese-style Italian food—not Japanese and Italian fusion food. Their pastas are made with Japanese ingredients, as are their pizzas, with mentaiko topping, melted mochi, uni (sea urchin), nori, and soy sauce. Imagine Italian cuisine you would expect to eat in Japan.

Miko Matsumaru

After opening a successful Japanese restaurant in Hollywood, Matsumaru expanded to Southbay, California, an area highly respected for its Asian cuisine.

About Yuzu Pepper Paste

Yuzu is an Asian citrus fruit, about the size of a grapefruit. It has a tart taste with background notes of Mandarin orange. When made into a paste, it gets mashed together with spicy chili peppers and salt that give dishes an instant flavor shot. Be careful, a little goes a long way!

SICHUAN DAN DAN NOODLES

Crunchy peanuts, carrots, and green onions give this dish a nice texture and taste

M.Y. CHINA

M.Y. China
845 Market Street, Level 4
San Francisco, CA 94103
(415) 580-3001

Cuisine: Chinese

Chef Martin Yan

M.Y. China offers authentic Chinese cuisine in a modern experience. Inspired by Chef Martin Yan and his years of teaching the art of Chinese cuisine, a full exhibition kitchen brings the ancient art of the wok, hand-pulled noodles, and dim sum to light.

Serves 4

For the Marinade:

2 tbsp Chinese rice wine

2 tbsp soy sauce

2 tsp cornstarch

6 oz/170 g ground pork

For the Sauce:

½ cup/120 ml sesame seed paste

3 tbsp chicken broth

2 tbsp oyster-flavored sauce

1 tbsp soy sauce

1 tbsp Chinkiang vinegar

1 tsp chili garlic sauce

1 tsp Sichuan peppercorn oil

1 tsp toasted sesame seeds

½ tsp sugar

12 oz/340 g fresh Chinese noodles

1 tbsp vegetable oil

¼ cup/50 g shredded Sichuan
    preserved vegetables

¼ cup/15 g thinly sliced green onion

¼ cup/40 g shredded cucumber

¼ cup/40 g shredded carrot

¼ cup/40 g chopped roasted, salted peanuts

Chef Martin Yan

The celebrated host of over 3,000 cooking shows broadcast worldwide, Martin Yan enjoys distinction as a certified Master Chef, a highly respected food consultant, a cooking instructor, and a prolific author.

1. Combine marinade ingredients in a bowl. Add pork and mix well. Let stand for 10 minutes.

2. Combine sauce ingredients in a separate bowl and whisk until smooth; set aside.

3. Bring a large pot of salted water to a boil. Cook noodles according to package directions. Drain, rinse with cold water, and drain again. Place noodles in a serving bowl.

4. Heat a wok over high heat. Add oil, swirling to coat sides. Add pork and stir-fry until cooked, about 2 minutes.

5. Add sauce and cook until heated through. Pour sauce over noodles. Top with preserved vegetables, green onion, cucumber, carrot, and peanuts.

STREET STYLE NOODLES

Pork belly and noodles that can be eaten on the run

Jum Mum

5 St. Mark's Place
New York, NY 10003
(212) 673-6903

Cuisine: Korean, Chinese, Asian Fusion

Chef Ian Kittichai

In January 2012 Chef Kittichai debuted to a 15 million fan following as one of the permanent Iron Chefs on the *Iron Chef Thailand* television show. In May of that year, he opened Jum Mum, an Asian bun eatery in New York City.

Serves 4

¼ cup/60 ml vegetable oil

4 lb/1.8 kg pork belly

1 cup/240 ml mushroom soy sauce

¾ cup/180 ml seasoning soy sauce

¾ cup/180 ml sweet soy sauce

10 black peppercorns

4 cloves garlic

3 cilantro roots

2 whole star anise

1 cinnamon stick

8 oz/230 g rice noodles, thick cut

4 oz/113 g smoked tofu, diced

4 oz/113 g scallions, chopped

1. Heat oil in a large, heavy skillet; brown pork belly on both sides until charred.

2. Transfer the pork belly to a large, heavy saucepan. Add mushroom soy sauce, seasoning soy sauce, sweet soy sauce, peppercorns, garlic, cilantro root, anise, and cinnamon stick. Bring the mixture to a boil for three hours until the pork is soft and tender. If liquid cooks down too much, add a light stock to keep pork covered while cooking.

3. Remove pork belly from the sauce and roughly chop. Keep warm.

4. Steam noodles in bamboo basket until hot. Arrange the noodles on plate, top with chopped pork belly and smoked tofu. Sprinkle chopped scallions on top.

Chef Ian Kittichai

Chef Ian Kittichai's path to culinary success started from very humble beginnings in Bangkok. Every morning he would rise at 3 a.m. to accompany his mother to the wet market to select the best meats, seafood, and vegetables for her neighborhood grocery. While Ian was at school, she would cook a dozen different types of curries. Upon his return home, Ian would push a cart through the neighborhood to sell his wares, shouting: "Khow Geang Ron Ron Ma Leaw Jaar!" (Hot curry coming!)

About Cilantro Root

Perhaps it's not the end you're familiar cooking with, but the root of the cilantro plant is a staple herb in lots of Asian dishes. It actually has a milder flavor than the leaves. The root can be washed and frozen without losing any of its potency.

TRADITIONAL PHO NOODLE SOUP WITH BEEF

A heartily spiced beef noodle soup

MUI NE
RESORT & SPA

Lanterns Restaurant

1 Pham Hong Thai Street
Hoi An City,
Quang Nam Province, Vietnam
84 510 391 4555

Cuisine: Vietnamese

Chef Thai Ngoc Hieu

Start your day at Lanterns with a delicious breakfast in the French colonial-style dining room with a wonderful river view. Return in the evening to find a menu that showcases the very best of Vietnamese cuisine.

Serves 1

10 oz/300 g beef bones

5 oz/150 g beef shank

1 oz/20 g fresh ginger

1 oz/20 g shallot

2 oz/50 g lemongrass

2 star anise

2 cinnamon sticks (1 in/2cm)

1 black cardamom

2 cloves

3½ oz/100 g beef fillet

Fish sauce

Salt

Pepper

Sugar

10 oz/300 g rice noodles, uncooked

1 cup/100 g soy sprouts

2 oz/50 g onions, sliced in rings

2 oz/50 g green onions, cut in 2 in/5 cm pieces

Fresh Herbs: peppermint, coriander and
smooth coriander, saw-tooth coriander,
to taste

Condiments: fish sauce, fresh chili, ground
pepper, chili sauce, black soy sauce

Chef Thai Ngoc Hieu

Hieu comes from Chau Doc, a town in the Mekong Delta. The area has many green rice fields and fruit plantations with mangosteen, rambutan, oranges, mangoes, and durians, which he says have inspired his creativity and passion for cooking. Before joining Anantara, Hieu had twelve years of experience cooking at various resorts around Vietnam. He is an expert in classic Vietnamese cuisines, such as Cha Gio (fresh spring rolls), Crispy Shrimp Wrapped Paper Rolls, Traditional Cham Pot Roasted Pork, and Duck.

1. Rinse the beef bones and beef shank and blanch them in boiling water for 2 minutes.

2. Roast ginger and shallots.

3. Put the beef bones and shank into a stockpot with 2 qt/2 L cold water and bring to a boil. When boiling, skim foam and reduce the heat to a simmer.

4. Add lemongrass, star anise, cinnamon sticks, cardamom, and cloves and the piece of beef filet. Simmer over low heat for about 3 hours (can also be cooked in a 400°F/200°C oven).

5. Take out beef filet and shank; drain well. Strain the stock, return to heat, and bring back to a boil.

6. Adjust seasoning to taste with fish sauce, salt, ground pepper and a bit of sugar.

7. Poach the noodles and soy sprouts in boiling water for two seconds, place in large bowl.

8. On top arrange finely sliced beef shank, beef fillet, onions, herbs, roasted ginger, and shallots.

9. Pour the very hot Pho consommé stock over the meat and vegetables. Serve condiments on the side.

VIETNAMESE BEEF STEW NOODLES

Long, slow cooking brings out deep flavors in this richly seasoned stew

BaoQi

620 Davie Street
Vancouver, British Columbia
V6B 2J5, Canada
(604) 700-4100

Cuisine: Vietnamese

Chef Kim Dieu Tran

Vietnamese comfort food is the fare at this family-owned and family-run restaurant featuring fresh ingredients and a pleasant dining experience.

Chef Kim Dieu Tran

Kim Dieu Tran worked at the U.S. Embassy in Saigon until it fell to the North Vietnamese, when she bought a boat and escaped from Vietnam to Thailand, losing almost everything to pirates along the way. She and her husband arrived in Canada in 1979 as refugees.

Serves 4

2 lb/900 g beef shank, cut into 1½ in/4 cm
    cubes

2 tbsp annato seed oil*

2 beef tendon strips or about 1/2 lb/230 g

1 stalk of lemongrass (white end bruised and
    sliced into 4-5 in/10-12 cm pieces)

3-4 star anise seeds, (toasted optional)

2 bay leaves

½ knob of ginger, thinly sliced

32 oz/950 ml beef broth

4 medium sized carrots, sliced

1 lb/450 g coooked rice noodles

For Spice Marinade:

1 tbsp diced shallots

1 tbsp minced garlic

1 tbsp paprika

1 tbsp minced lemongrass

½ tbsp fish sauce

½ tsp red chili powder

¼ tsp cinnamon

¼ tsp clove powder

¼ tsp anise powder

1 tsp ground pepper

1 tsp sugar

Accompaniments:

Toasted French baguettes

Fresh basil

Pickled onions

Lime/lemon wedges

Diced cilantro and green onions

Sliced jalapeños

1. In large mixing bowl, combine the beef shank with the spice marinade for at least 2 hours.

2. Sauté the beef with 1 tbsp of annato seed oil over medium high heat until browned and seared. Transfer this into a slow cooker.

3. Add the beef tendons, lemongrass, star anise seeds, bay leaves, ginger, and beef broth. You may need to add more broth or water to just cover and submerge the beef.

4. Set slow cooker to lowest possible setting and allow to cook uncovered overnight or for about eight hours.

5. About 1 hour before it's done, add the carrots. Just before serving, add remaining 1 tbsp of annato seed oil to the broth for a great red color. Make final adjustment and season to taste.

6. Serve over noodles with accompaniments according to your taste.

*To make annatto seed oil, heat 2 tbsp olive oil with ½ tbsp annato seeds. The oil will be steeped with a red color. Do not allow oil to boil. When the color is steeped red, turn off heat and drain the seeds.

VIETNAMESE GRILLED LEMONGRASS PORK BUN

This healthier version of a traditional pork noodle
recipe requires some advance preparation

BT

EAT LOCAL - THINK GLOBAL

BT

2507 South MacDill Avenue #B
Tampa, FL 33629
(813) 258-1916

Cuisine: French-Vietnamese

Chef BT Nguyen

BT is a gourmet restaurant with an international flavor, most
notably its distinctive French-Vietnamese hybrid dishes.

Chef BT Nguyen

BT's obsession with the kitchen began as a child in
Vietnam. At the fall of Saigon, a young BT began a long
journey finally ending in the United States. After college,
she continued her passion for cooking while pursuing
a career in the fashion industry. Ultimately, BT left the
fashion industry to become a restaurateur.

Serves 6-8

For the Pork:

For the Marinade:
2 tbsp pure Japanese sesame oil
3 tsp soy sauce
2 tsp minced shallots
2 tsp minced garlic
1 tsp freshly ground pepper
2 tsp fish sauce (the best quality)
2 tbsp palm sugar
2 tbsp minced lemongrass
1 tsp five-spice powder

1½ lb/680 g lean pork loin, thinly sliced (about ¼ inch/.5 cm)

1. Combine all the marinade ingredients in a large bowl. Add pork and mix well.

2. Then cover and refrigerator for at least 2-3 hours.

3. Grill pork until slightly charred.

For Pickled Carrots and Daikon:
1 large carrot, julienned
1 daikon, julienned
1 cup/240 ml rice vinegar
½ cup/120 ml water
½ cup/100 g sugar
½ cup/ 120 g salt

1. Place carrots and daikon in a container.

2. Mix vinegar, water, sugar, and salt and pour over vegetables to cover. Refrigerate for at least 2 hours.

For Vietnamese Dipping Sauce:
4 cloves garlic, minced
2 fresh chili peppers, chopped
2 tbsp palm sugar
1 tbsp rice vinegar
Juice of 2 limes
½ cup/120 ml fish sauce
½ cup/120 ml coconut water (or coconut soda)

Mix all ingredients together and set aside.

To Assemble:

1 package dry rice vermicelli noodles
Lettuce and herb salad mix: thinly chopped lettuce, mint, perilla, basil, bean sprouts, diced cucumber
1 cup/160 g roasted unsalted peanuts, coarsely crushed
Scallion Oil: 1 cup/60 g chopped scallions mixed with ½ cup/120 ml olive oil
Roasted shallots, to taste

1. Cook noodles in boiling water for 8-10 minutes, stirring frequently so they won't stick to the bottom of the pot. Drain and rinse under cold running water.

2. In a bowl place the lettuce and herb salad mix.

3. Spread the noodles on top.

4. Add the peanuts, pickled daikon and carrots, scallions in oil, roasted shallots, and grilled pork.

5. Pour dipping sauce over all.

VIETNAMESE SAUSAGE ON LICORICE STICKS WITH CHILLED RICE VERMICELLI SALAD

Unusual flavor combination with a very unique presentation

Chef Matt Rojas

For Chef Matt Rojas, cooking began at a young age in the mountains of Arizona. He spent frequent hours in the kitchen with his mother and grandmother, learning initial techniques that he still uses to this day. His love for the culinary world heightened during hunting and fishing trips with his family where Chef Rojas experimented with campfire cookery, foraging and butchery. Every food experience inspired him. Following high school he attended the Art Institute of Phoenix and the years after were spent staging and working in Scottsdale, San Francisco, and finally New York. Nine years were spent in professional kitchens before he achieved his goal of becoming an executive chef when he was retained at Rouge et Blanc. In 2011, the restaurant received a two star rating in *The New York Times*. Chef Rojas received a nomination from fellow chefs to be included in the *Best Chefs of America* 2013 edition.

Serves 8

For Vietnamese Sausage:

For Sausage Mix:
2 cups/120 g green onions
¼ cup/60 ml honey
½ cup/120 ml fish sauce
½ cup/80 g garlic, chopped
2 tbsp pepper
Scant 1 oz/20 g Thai chilies
1 oz/30 g lemongrass
6½ oz/100 g ume paste
⅕ oz/5 g oregano, parsley and mint mix
5 lb/2.25 kg ground pork, 30% fat
16 licorice sticks 6 in/15 cm in length

1. Pulse all sausage mix ingredients in a food processor to a smooth consistency.
2. Mix with ground pork using your hands.
3. Wrap around licorice sticks and refrigerate.
4. When ready to cook, grill or sauté in a pan for 6-8 minutes, or until cooked through, turning constantly.

For Rice Vermicelli Noodle Salad:
4 cups/360 g cooked rice vermicelli noodles
1 cup/100 g bean sprouts, blanched
1 cup/150 g cucumbers, julienned
½ cup/35 g mint, minced
½ cup/30 g scallions, chopped
¼ cup/60 ml lemon juice

Garnish:
Toasted pistachios
Sunflower sprouts

1. Toss all salad ingredients in a bowl and refrigerate.
2. When ready to serve, add Sweet Vidalia Onion Vinaigrette (recipe below) to taste and toss to mix.
3. Garnish with pistachios and sunflower sprouts.
4. Divide salad among eights plates.
4. Put two cooked sausage sticks on top of salad on each plate.

Sweet Vidalia Onion Vinaigrette

4 cups/640 g Vidalia onion, large dice
½ cup/120 ml rice wine vinegar
½ cup/120 ml soy sauce
1 tsp fresh ground black pepper
½ cup/120 ml grapeseed oil
¼ cup/60 ml sesame oil

Emulsify all ingredients in a blender and refrigerate.

WINTER MELON AND PORK RIB SOUP WITH VERMICELLI

The melon imparts a fresh flavor to this pork noodle soup

Serves 4-5

2½ lb/1 kg rack of pork ribs

1½ oz/45 ml fish sauce

1 small onion

1 small knob of ginger

1 piece of kombu (optional)

2 tbsp coriander seeds

1 tbsp black peppercorns

4 tbsp bonito flakes (optional)

4 oz/113 g dried shrimp

2 lb/900 g winter melon

1 lb/450 g vermicelli rice noodles

Handful of cilantro (de-stemmed)

3 tbsp thinly sliced green onions

1. Parboil rack of pork ribs for 1 minute. Rinse pot and pork. Refill pot with 7 qt/6.5 L of water and bring to a simmer. Trim individual pork ribs, leaving a bit of meat on bone. Excess meat can be butchered down to bite size pieces. Put both into simmering pot. Add fish sauce.

2. Char small onion and ginger over flame for a few minutes each. Rinse both and place in broth for 15 minutes and discard.

3. Place kombu in broth and simmer for 30 minutes and discard. Toast coriander and black peppercorn until fragrant but not burnt. Wrap toasted coriander and black peppercorns with bonito flakes and dried shrimp in cheesecloth, and place in simmering broth.

4. Simmer broth for at least 2 hours, periodically skimming off the fat.

5. Skin winter melon. Cut in half lengthwise and scoop out the seeds. Cut melon in ⅓ inch/1 cm slices. Simmer winter melon in broth for 8 minutes or until slightly tender.

6. Boil vermicelli rice noodles for 5 minutes until al dente. Strain and place in large soup bowls.

7. Distribute pork and winter melon in soup bowls and ladle in hot broth through a strainer. Garnish with a handful of cilantro and scallions.

8. Happy Eating.

An Choi

85 Orchard St.
New York, NY 10002
(212) 226-3700

Cuisine: Vietnamese

Chef Matt Le-Khac

An Choi is a Vietnamese eatery located in the heart of the Lower East Side. An Choi brings the streetside frenetic thrill of Saigon hustle and bustle into a dining experience within its neon lit, Vietnamese-propaganda covered walls. Every night, New York's downtown crowd of designers, creatives, and foodies alike take advantage of the energy and bring their friends to An Choi (eat and play) and in true Vietnamese fashion have a drink along with their bowl of pho.

Chef Matt Le-Khac

Le-Khac didn't start cooking Vietnamese food until he left his home in Pennsylvania, where his father grew Asian herbs and vegetables. He describes his biggest challenge as obtaining the authentic fresh vegetables and spices that are essential to Vietnamese cuisine.

YAKIUDON

Sautéed pork belly and vegetables with noodles in a mild sauce.

Serves 1

For Yakiudon sauce:
½ cup/120 ml mirin
⅓ cup/80 ml soy sauce
A pinch of dashi powder

½ lb/230 g udon noodles
¼ cup/60g of cabbage
¼ cup/30g of onion
½ oz/10g of carrot
1/ 4 cup/30g of green bell pepper
Oil
⅛ lb/50g pork belly, sliced
¾ cup/80g bean sprouts
Bonito flakes
Cut nori

1   Prepare the yakiudon sauce and set aside.

2.   Bring a pot of water to a boil for the udon noodles and cook until done.

3.   Cut the cabbage, onion, carrot, and pepper in bite-sized pieces.

4.   Put a little vegetable oil in a pan and heat it up. When hot, add the pork, onion, carrot, and cabbage.

5.   When the vegetables are cooked, add the bean sprouts and green bell pepper.

6.   Add the boiled udon noodles to the frying pan, mixing them with the vegetables. Add sauce little by little, to your taste.

7.   Put on a plate and garnish with bonito flakes and cut nori.

MADAKE

Imadake

4006 Sainte-Catherine Street West
Westmount, QC H3Z 1P2
Canada
(514) 931-8833

Cuisine: Japanese

Chef Mineho Okunishi

Imadake strives to give everyone an authentic Japanese Izakaya experience. This extends to every aspect of the restaurant from the recipes and chefs to the sakes and the music. They believe that business should not come at the expense of the environment. All the ingredients are environmentally sustainable. The meats and vegetables are organic and the seafoods follow the "OceanWise" guidelines. Imadake recycles and uses energy-efficient appliances to lower the impact on nature.

Chef Mineho Okunishi

Chef Mineho Okunishi has worked in various restaurants in Japan over a period of ten years, and has experience in different kinds of cooking, from kaiseki to izakaya. His vision for Imadake's menu is being able to experience the taste of a real Japanese izakaya in Montreal without having to set foot in Japan.

POULTRY

ASIAN CHICKEN NOODLE SALAD

Crisp veggies and tender noodles tossed with a garlic-ginger
infused dressing with notes of lime and honey

Gluten Free Spinner

www.glutenfreespinner.com

Chef Mary Brueske

Chef Mary Brueske

Chef Mary Brueske's favorite pastime is
enjoying time with her family and friends,
which usually includes gathering in her home
with a spread of great food and wine, sharing
music, laughter, and the simple pleasure of being
together.

The name Gluten Free Spiiner came from Chef Brueske's huband asking, "What are you spinning-up
tonight?" in reference to continuous attempts at creating new recipes while spinning the spice wheel to add
another flavor. The "gluten free" designator came in December 2009 when she learned she had a gluten
intolerance and became a gluten-free girl. Although the journey was challenging at first, Chef Brueske notes
that the health benefits have been remarkable.

She learned that many products contain gluten and that there was a long list of "old staples" she would need
to replace.

Now her kitchen is gluten-free. She has learned to cook glueten-free as she did before, enjoying the food, its
preparation, and the final result. She re-created many of her favorite recipes to be gluten-free, and as she did,
she learned new ways to use other products to produce the same result. She also researched the many online
blogs and celiac sites to educate herself on living gluten-free, and she is grateful to the pioneers of a gluten-
free lifestyle, as they created the awareness of the tools available. Many grocers are beginning to carry organic,
gluten-free products, and the challenge is now minimal.

Serves 4

4 oz/113 g brown rice noodles

1 ½/ tk g cups cooked shredded chicken breast

1 cup/340 g shredded cabbage

¼ cup/15 g chopped green onions

2 tbsp chopped cilantro leaves or mint leaves

½ cup/170 g matchstick carrots

2 celery stalks, cut on an angle

1 red bell pepper, seeded and sliced into strips
    (use ½ if a large pepper)

Garnish:

Pea pods sliced lengthwise

Seedless cucumber, sliced in 2-in/5-cm strips

Toasted almond slices or cashews

1. Cook noodles according to package
    directions. Drain and rinse well under cold
    water.

2. In a large glass bowl, toss together the
    noodles, chicken, and vegetables and
    gradually add the prepared dressing, a
    little at a time, while tossing to coat all
    ingredients. You may not need all the
    dressing, so don't add all at once.

3. Garnish with peapods, cucumber, and
    almonds or cashews. Chill until ready
    to serve.

Ginger Honey Dressing

¼ cup/60 ml hoisin sauce

1 tbsp pickled ginger, chopped

1 tsp chopped garlic

1 tbsp rice vinegar

1 tbsp gluten-free soy sauce

4 tbsp canola oil

2 tsp sesame oil

2-3 tbsp water (to desired consistency)

1 tsp hot chili sauce

1 tbsp honey

Juice from ½ lime

Whisk together the dressing ingredients until
thoroughly combined.

ASIAN CHICKEN AND NOODLES

Asian flavor in a flash

Serves 4

8 oz/230 g medium egg noodles, uncooked

1 tbsp vegetable or olive oil

1 lb/450 g boneless, skinless chicken breasts, cut into julienne strips

2 carrots, peeled and thinly sliced

1 bunch green onions, chopped

½ red bell pepper, thinly sliced

¼ cup/60 ml low-sodium soy sauce

3 stalks celery, chopped

1 4-oz/113-g can sliced water chestnuts

½ tsp garlic powder

½ tsp white pepper

1 tsp dried cilantro

2 tbsp toasted almonds (optional)

1. Prepare egg noodles according to package directions; drain.

2. Heat oil in a large skillet or wok. Add chicken, carrots, green onions, and red bell pepper and sauté until chicken is opaque and white, about 4 minutes, stirring constantly.

3. Add soy sauce, celery, water chestnuts, garlic powder, white pepper, and cilantro. Mix all ingredients together, cover, and simmer for 5 minutes.

4. Stir in cooked egg noodles. Sprinkle with toasted almonds, if desired.

National Pasta Association

750 National Press Building
529 14th Street, NW
Washington, DC 20045
(202) 591-2459

The National Pasta Association (NPA) is the trade association for the United States pasta industry. The leading resource for all things pasta, NPA was founded in 1904 and is comprised of manufacturing, industry suppliers, and allied industry representatives. For more information, recipes, or cooking tips, please visit www.pastafits.org.

About Water Chestnuts

Actually, water chestnuts are not nuts at all. They are, however, grown under water. Water chestnuts are an aquatic vegetable usually found in marshes. The "chestnut" is under the mud and tall, leafless green stems are what show above the water. The unusual makeup of a water chestnut's cell walls give it its most prized characteristic: It stays crisp and crunchy even after cooking or canning.

ASIAN CHICKEN PASTA SALAD

A cold salad with chicken and spinach that's perfect for a hot summer night

Serves 4

8 oz/230 g orzo, small shells, or other small
    pasta shape, uncooked

2 cups/460 g poached chicken, cut into chunks

4 oz/113 g spinach leaves (remove stems), and
    sliced into strips

½ cup/50 g bean sprouts

½ red bell pepper, ribs removed and cut
    into strips

2 green onions, sliced

3 tbsp red wine vinegar

1 tbsp reduced-sodium soy sauce

1 tbsp sesame or vegetable oil

2 tsp teriyaki sauce

1½ tbsp prepared chili sauce

1 tbsp fresh grated ginger

3 tbsp slivered almonds, toasted

1. Prepare pasta according to package
   directions; drain.

2. In large mixing bowl, combine pasta,
   chicken, spinach, sprouts, pepper, and
   green onions.

3. In a small mixing bowl, whisk together
   remaining ingredients except almonds.

4. Toss dressing with pasta mixture and
   refrigerate until ready to serve. Sprinkle
   almonds over top just before serving.

National Pasta Association

750 National Press Building
529 14th Street, NW
Washington, DC 20045
(202) 591-2459

The National Pasta Association (NPA) is the trade
association for the United States pasta industry. The leading
resource for all things pasta, NPA was founded in 1904
and is comprised of manufacturing, industry suppliers,
and allied industry representatives. For more information,
recipes, or cooking tips, please visit www.pastafits.org.

BOW TIES WITH ASIAN CHICKEN

Asian flavor with staples found in most pantries

Serves 6

1 lb/450 g bow ties, mostaccioli or other medium pasta shape, uncooked

4 tbsp low-sodium soy sauce

2 tbsp honey

2 tbsp lime juice

3 tsp Dijon mustard with seeds

1 lb/450 g boneless, skinless chicken breasts, cut into ½ in/1 cm cubes

½ cup/120 ml chicken broth or pasta cooking liquid *

2 small red bell peppers, cored, seeded, and thinly sliced lengthwise

6 green onions, trimmed and thinly sliced

Freshly ground pepper

4 tbsp chopped fresh parsley

1. Prepare pasta according to package directions. Drain thoroughly in a colander and return the pasta to the pot.

2. Stir the soy sauce, honey, lime juice, and mustard in a small bowl until the honey is dissolved. Add the chicken pieces and turn until coated with the marinade. Refrigerate for 30 minutes.

3. Transfer the chicken and marinade to a large, nonstick skillet. Cook over medium heat until chicken is cooked through, about 4 minutes. Remove from the heat and pour in the chicken broth (or reserved pasta water).

4. Add the contents of the skillet, the red peppers, and the scallions to the pot with the pasta. Heat to simmering over low heat. Toss the pasta once or twice, add ground pepper to taste, and divide among serving bowls. Sprinkle each serving with chopped fresh parsley.

    * If you do not have chicken broth, ladle off and reserve ½ cup/120 ml pasta cooking liquid just before draining the pasta.

National Pasta Association

750 National Press Building
529 14th Street, NW
Washington, DC 20045
(202) 591-2459

The National Pasta Association (NPA) is the trade association for the United States pasta industry. The leading resource for all things pasta, NPA was founded in 1904 and is comprised of manufacturing, industry suppliers, and allied industry representatives. For more information, recipes, or cooking tips, please visit www.pastafits.org.

CHIANG MAI NOODLES

This rich soup packs some spicy curry heat

Doc Chey's Noodle House

1556 N Decatur Road
Atlanta, GA 30307
(404) 378-8188

Two other locations in Atlanta
and another in Asheville, NC

Cuisine: Pan Asian

Chef Rich Chey

Doc Chey's approach to food is simple—prepare it fresh; make it from
scratch; and only use the freshest, finest ingredients.

Chef Rich Chey

The idea for Doc Chey's came over sixteen years ago during Rich Chey's
travels throughout Asia. "I really enjoyed Japan because of the Ramen houses
and the role they play in society. They are the diners of Japan, where people go
for delicious freshly prepared food that is affordable and served quickly." Chey
and Brook Messina opened the first Doc Chey's in 1997.

Serves 2

For Pickled Veggies:

1 cup/240 ml water

½ cup/120 ml white vinegar

½ cup/100 g sugar

1 tbsp kosher salt

1 cup/150 g carrots, shredded

1 cup/340 g green cabbage, shredded

½ cup/30 g green onions, cut in 1 in/2.5 cm pieces

1. Combine water, vinegar, sugar and salt and mix until salt and sugar are dissolved. Add carrots, cabbage, and green onions to pickling liquid and place in refrigerator for at least two hours. Mix occasionally until veggies wilt and are fully covered by pickling liquid.

For Curry Soup:

¼ cup/60 ml vegetable oil

¼ cup/60 ml red curry paste

2 tbsp yellow curry powder

¾ tsp ground cumin

½ lb/230 g raw chicken, cut in 1 in/2.5 cm pieces

3 cans coconut cream

1 qt/950 ml chicken stock

¼ cup/60 ml fish sauce

3 tbsp white sugar

1 red pepper, chopped small

2 green onions, thinly sliced

1. Combine red curry paste, yellow curry powder, and ground cumin in stockpot and heat until spices become fragrant.

2. Add the chicken to the curry mixture and stir to coat the chicken with curry. Cook until the outside of the chicken is seared.

3. Add coconut cream, chicken stock, and bring contents to a boil. Turn down heat and simmer for 30 minutes.

4. Add fish sauce and sugar and mix until sugar is dissolved.

5. Add red peppers and green onions. Cover pot and let stand for 5 minutes.

2 cups/115 g egg noodles

½ cup/80 g pickled cabbage

1 tbsp chili oil

2 tbsp chopped cilantro

Lime wedge

1. Cook egg noodles and divide among soup bowls. Ladle curry soup and contents into each bowl.

2. Garnish soup with pickled cabbage, chili oil, cilantro, and lime. Serve with Pickled Veggies.

CHICKEN HAKKA NOODLES

A one-dish dinner with chicken, vegetables and noodles

Serves 4

12 oz/340 g hakka noodles
  (flat egg noodles)

1 lb/450 g chicken breast

Soy sauce, for marinating

2 tbsp peanut oil

2 eggs

Pinch of salt

4 clove garlic, minced

2 green chilies, stemmed and split

4 oz/113 g green cabbage, shredded

1 large carrot, julienned

1 small green bell pepper, julienned

1 small red bell pepper, julienned

Salt to taste

2 tsp soy sauce

1 tsp white vinegar

½ tsp white pepper

2 oz/60 g bean sprouts

4 green onions, three cut on the
    diagonal in 1 in/2.5 cm pieces;
    one thinly sliced for garnish

Chef Jayanta Kishore Paul

Paul came to Los Angeles from Mumbai, where he was executive chef at a five-star hotel and catered to royals, high-ranking politicians, industry leaders, and Bollywood celebrities. He was lured to the US to open a Beverly Hills restaurant, which, after just six months, was named Best Indian Restaurant in Los Angeles. A perfectionist about ingredients, proportions, and cooking methods, Paul even makes and grinds his own fresh spices. "Being a master chef," he says, "takes more than talent and training. It also requires equal parts of working hard and loving what you do."

1. Boil the noodles in salted water till al dente. Strain and spread on a kitchen towel to remove the extra moisture.

2. Clean chicken breast and cut into thin strips. Marinate in soy sauce to cover for 15 minutes.

3. Heat 1 tbsp oil in a skillet. Sauté the chicken until done and keep aside.

4. Beat the eggs with a pinch of salt and make a thin omelette in a wok. Cut the omelette into thin strips and set aside.

5. Heat remaining 1 tbsp oil in a wok over high heat. Add chopped garlic and sauté till fragrant.

6. Add chilies, sauté for 15 seconds. Add cabbage and carrots, stir-fry for a minute. Add bell peppers and toss.

7. Then add the noodles, salt, soy sauce, vinegar and pepper. Stir-fry for one more minute.

8. Now add the chicken, strips of omelette, bean sprouts and green onion pieces. Stir-fry and mix well. Correct the seasoning and serve hot garnished with thinly sliced scallions.

DUCK NOODLE SOUP

Good on cold winter nights

Serves 4-6

Chinese herbal soup mix (available in Chinese
  groceries)
Palo powder packet
1 duck
White and dark soy sauces
Salt
Sugar
1 lb/450 g rice noodles
Green chili pickle in vinegar
Chili powder
Fish sauce

Garnish:
Bean sprouts
Green onion stems, chopped
Chinese celery (cilantro)
Deep-fried garlic

1. Bring a large pot of water to a boil. Stir in
    soup mix and Palo powder.

2. Put duck into the pot and turn heat down
    to medium. Simmer duck for about 1 hour
    and then remove from pot.

3. Taste broth and adjust flavor with white
    and dark soy sauces, salt, and sugar.

4. Cook noodles in boiling water until soft.
    Drain and set aside.

5. Transfer noodles to serving bowl. Cut up
    cooked duck and add pieces to the bowl.

6. Pour duck broth over noodles and duck.
    Adjust taste with sugar, green chili pickle,
    chili powder, fish sauce.

7. Garnish with bean sprouts, green onions,
    cilantro, and fried garlic.

Thai Thai Cafe

13605 Roscoe Boulevard
Panorama City, CA 91402
(818) 786-2233

Cuisine: Thai

Chef Niasporn Komolha

Chef Nisaporn Komolha

Niasporn grew up in Thailand and wanted to bring
healthy and delicious Thai cuisine to America.
After selling her food at farmer's markets across
Los Angeles and being a private chef, she decided
it was time to open Thai Thai Cafe.

FIVE-SPICED DUCK MEATBALLS AND NOODLES

Lacinato kale and smoked chili add health benefits and rich flavor to this dish

revel

Revel

403 N. 36th Street
Seattle, WA 98103
(206) 547-2040

Cuisine: Korean

Chefs Rachel Yang and Seif Chirchi

Learn how to make Revel's dishes with the chefs in hands-on classes that are held right in the restaurant.

Serves 6

For Duck Meatballs:

2 lb/900 g duck leg meat, ground

1 tbsp five-spice powder

1 tbsp orange zest

3 tbsp soy sauce

¼ cup/35 g daikon, brunoise, pickled

¼ cup/40 g black currant, pickled

¼ cup/40 g onion, brunoise, sweated

For the Sauce:

½ cup/120 ml housemade smoked chili or sambal

½ cup/120 ml sake

½ cup/120 ml mirin

¾ cup/180 ml soy sauce

4 tbsp butter

24 oz/680 g udon noodles

2 bunches lacinato kale, coarsely chopped

¼ cup/20 g duck cracklings

¼ cup/8 g cilantro

2 tbsp pickled ginger, julienned

1. Mix the duck meat with the rest of the meatball ingredients. Shape into meatballs.

2. Mix all ingredients for the sauce and set aside.

3. Cook the noodles and reserve.

4. Brown the meatballs and add the sauce and reduce.

5. Add the kale and noodles.

6. Serve with duck cracklings, cilantro, and pickled ginger.

About the chefs

Husband and wife chef duo Rachel Yang and Seif Chirchi met while cooking at New York's illustrious Alain Ducasse at the Essex House. While both chefs have a distinctly different point of view, their tastes blend together to create modern, creative, and seamless cuisine in their restaurants, Joule and Revel. Rachel's Korean heritage informs her flavors through her impeccable training in classic French technique. Seif, raised in Chicago, and trained in Portland, OR, brings a distinctly American flavor to the palate, balancing and complementing his wife both in the kitchen and at home.

GRILLED LEMONGRASS CHICKEN VERMICELLI BOWL

Asian flavor with staples found in most pantries

Saigon Kitchen

526 West State Street
Ithaca, NY 14850
(607) 257-8881

Cuisine: Vietnamese

Chefs Bill Lam and
Phouc Tran

The Lam family opened the doors to Saigon Kitchen in 2011 to introduce authentic Vietnamese food to Ithaca, New York. With the belief that great food and cooking brings family, friends and loved ones together, the Lam family took a chance and opened what is now one of the hottest places to grab a bite in Ithaca—a restaurant that is home to foodies and adventurous diners.

Serves 4

For Lemongrass Marinated Chicken:

2 lb/900 g boneless chicken breast

4 tbsp soy sauce

3 tbsp honey

2 tbsp sugar

3 tbsp ground fresh lemongrass

1 garlic clove, smashed

2 tbsp green onions, white parts

2 tbsp cornstarch

2 tbsp vegetable oil

1½ cups/135 g shredded iceberg or romaine lettuce

Bean sprouts

1 cucumber, julienned

32 oz/900 g cooked vermicelli rice noodle

Garnish:

4 tbsp crushed peanuts

4 tbsp green onions

Pickled carrots

Nuoc Mam dressing (recipe below)

1. Slice the chicken lengthwise, approximately ¼ in/.5 cm thick, and set aside.

2. In a small bowl combine soy sauce, honey, sugar, lemongrass, garlic, and green onions, and whisk until smooth.

3. Pour the marinade over the chicken and evenly coat all the pieces of chicken.

4. Add cornstarch to the chicken marinade mixture and combine well.

5. Add oil to the chicken marinade mixture and make sure everything is evenly coated.

6. Cover and let chicken marinate for at least 1 hour and up to 12 hours for maximum flavor.

7. Arrange four bowls with lettuce, bean sprouts, cucumber, and vermicelli noodles.

8. Prepare a medium-hot fire for direct heat grilling. Transfer the marinated chicken on to the grill and cook, turning once, approximately 3 minutes on each side, until the chicken is cooked through.

9. Arrange chicken on top of the vermicelli noodle and vegetable bowls. Top with peanuts and green onions. Serve with Nuoc Mam Dressing.

Nuoc Mam Dressing:

12 tbsp water

6 tbsp sugar

1 tsp sambal

2 tbsp vinegar

4 tbsp fish sauce

1 clove garlic, minced

Bring water, sugar, sambal, and vinegar to a boil until everything is dissolved. Immediately remove from heat and let cool to room temperature. Whisk in fish sauce and garlic. Keep refrigerated up to one week.

KHAO SOI KAI

Northern-style chicken curry with noodles

Sala Mae Nam

Golden Triangle Elephant
Camp and Resort
229 Moo 1, Chiang Saen
Chiang Rai 57150
Thailand
66 53 784 084

Cuisine: Thai

Chef Thai Ngoc Hieu

Feast on traditional northern Thai food
on a magnificent terrace covered by a lofty
ceiling and surrounded by dramatic views
of Thailand, Myanmar, and Laos.

Serves 1

8 oz/200 g northern or yellow egg noodles

1½ tbsp oil

1 oz/30 g red curry paste

½ can coconut milk

2 ½ tsp/5 g hung-lay powder (northern curry
        spice made from cumin and tumeric)

8 oz/200 g chicken breast

2½ tsp sugar

1 tbsp soy sauce

1 tbsp fish sauce

Chicken stock, to taste

⅛ cup/5 g green onions, sliced

3 tbsp/5 g coriander

1 oz/20 g yellow egg noodle, fried until crispy

Condiments:

1 oz/20 g pickled cabbage

1 oz/20 g shallots, finely chopped

1 oz/20 g chili flakes, fried

Lemons or limes, halved

Chef Thai Ngoc Hieu

Hieu comes from Chau Doc, a town in the Mekong Delta. The area has many green rice fields and fruit plantations such as mangosteen, rambutan, oranges, mangoes, and durians, which he says have inspired his creativity and passion in cooking.

Before joining Anantara, Hieu had twelve years of experience cooking at various resorts around Vietnam and is an expert in classic Vietnamese cuisines.

1. Bring a pot of water to a boil and add egg noodles. Cook for one minute. Drain and put in a bowl.

2. Heat the oil in a pan and fry red curry paste until it releases a nice aroma.

3. Add coconut milk and hung-lay powder; cook until the mixture thickens slightly.

4. Add chicken, sugar, soy sauce, fish sauce, and chicken stock to desired consistency and flavor. Simmer until the chicken is cooked.

5. Pour curry on top of noodles. Top with green onions, coriander, and crispy noodles. Serve condiments on the side.

RICE NOODLES WITH SHREDDED CHICKEN

It's a soup, it's a salad—it's both

CHAYA
BRASSERIE

Chaya

Multiple California locations in
Beverly Hills, Venice, Downtown LA,
and San Francisco

Cuisine: Franco-Japonaise

Chef Shigefumi Tachibe

The Chaya restaurant family originated when Hikage Chaya
opened in Hayama, Japan, over 400 years ago. From this initial
tea house, the Tsunoda family has expanded into French bistros
and pastry shops throughout Japan, to Chaya Brasserie Los
Angeles, Chaya Downtown, Chaya Venice, and Chaya Brasserie
San Francisco. The cuisine at all four restaurants can best be
described as French and Italian cuisine with a Japanese flair,
but each restaurant has a distinct personality reflecting its
own location. The most important tenet of the Chaya business
philosophy is hospitality, bringing the Japanese teahouse
tradition of warm and personal service to each and every guest.

Serves 2

8 oz/230 g dry rice noodles

3 cups/720 ml chicken broth (mirepoix
    in chicken stock)

8 oz/230 g shredded cooked chicken breast

2 star anise

For Herb Salad:

2 green onions, thinly sliced

10 mint leaves

½ a bundle of enoki mushrooms

½ red bell pepper, julienned

6 basil leaves

2 turnips, quartered

1. Cook the rice noodles in a pot of water for 2 to 3 minutes or until they're a chewy consistency, and set aside. Do not overcook.

2. Heat the broth in a medium saucepan. Add the shredded chicken and star anise. Bring to a boil.

3. Simmer for two minutes or until chicken is heated through.

4. Pour over prepared rice noodles in a bowl and top with herb salad.

Chef Shigefumi Tachibe

Chef Tachibe began training in formal French technique at the age of fifteen at the Hotel Ban Show Row in Nagasaki, Japan. He then served as an exchange chef at the restaurant Gannino in Milan, Italy, at the age of 21. Upon returning to Japan, he was named Executive Chef at La Marée de Chaya in Hayama, Japan. His experience with French and Italian cooking coupled with Japanese cuisine became the fusion that is now synonymous with Chaya Restaurants in California.

About Star Anise

It's the fruit of the Chinese magnolia tree found in Vietnam and southern China. With a licorice scent and taste, it's sweet and sharp at the same time, and of course with its star shape it's a pretty as well as flavorful addition to any dish. In Chinese medicine it is seen as a digestive aid.

SPICY CHICKEN AND UDON SOUP

This Asian dish has Mexican overtones using lime, avocado, and cilantro

Serves 4

2 tbsp olive oil

¼ cup/40 g red onion (small dice)

¼ cup/40 g celery (small dice)

¼ cup/40 g carrot (small dice)

¼ cup/45 g red pepper (small dice)

1 tbsp garlic, minced

1 tbsp jalapeño (fine dice)

1 qt/950 ml chicken stock

2 lb/900 g chicken (cooked and meat cut into small pieces)

2 tbsp green onions, thinly sliced

1 tbsp cilantro, chopped

1 lb/450 g udon noodles, cooked

Kosher salt & black pepper

2 tsp sesame oil

1 avocado, peeled & cut into medium chunks

1 lime, cut into quarters

1. Heat the olive oil in a saucepan to medium high heat. Add the onion, celery, carrot, red pepper, garlic, and jalapeño. Sauté for five minutes.

2. Add stock, chicken meat, green onions, cilantro, and noodles. Season with salt and pepper to taste.

3. Bring to a boil; then immediately lower to simmer for five minutes.

4. To serve: Divide hot soup into four hot bowls. Drizzle the sesame oil on top. Divide the avocado among the four bowls and serve each with a lime quarter.

Poco

33 Avenue B
New York, NY 10009
(212) 673-6903

Cuisine: Eclectic

Chef Walter Hinds

Chef Walter Hinds

Hinds weaves many international flavors into the very varied menu at Poco Restaurant. The cultural inspiration for this dish is Vietnamese.

About Limes

This common citrus fruit turns up frequently in southeast Asian recipes. Often it is used as a condiment or squeezed over dishes at the end of cooking time. To get the maximum amount of juice out of a lime, it should be at room temperature; roll it back and forth under the palm of your hand on a hard surface a few times to break down some of the fibers. Alternatively, you can microwave it for about 30 seconds.

TERIYAKI NOODLE STIR-FRY

Soba noodles or whole wheat linguine can be used in this chicken dish

The Six O'Clock Scramble

www.thescramble.com

Chef Aviva Goldfarb

Serves 6

8 oz/230 g Japanese soba noodles (or use whole wheat linguine)

4 tbsp vegetable oil

1 lb/450 g boneless, skinless chicken breasts or extra-firm tofu packed in water (cut the chicken into ½-in/1-cm strips or dice the tofu)

1 red, orange, or yellow bell pepper, cut into 1-in/2.5-cm strips strips

3 carrots, thinly sliced

1 small red onion, halved top to bottom and cut into thin half rings

3 green onions, green and white parts, sliced

¼ tsp crushed red pepper flakes (optional)

2 tbsp reduced-sodium soy sauce

4 tbsp reduced-sodium teriyaki or stir-fry sauce, or more to taste

Chef Aviva Goldfarb

Aviva Goldfarb is a family-dinner expert who helps busy parents let go of all the stress at 6:00 and bring joy and good nutrition back to the dinner table. She is a mother of two and the author and founder of The Six O'Clock Scramble, www.thescramble.com, an online dinner planning system and cookbook (St. Martin's Press, 2006), and is author of *SOS! The Six O'Clock Scramble to the Rescue: Earth Friendly, Kid-Pleasing Meals for Busy Families* (St. Martin's Press, 2010), which was named one of the best cookbooks of 2010 by *The Washington Post*. She is also a weekly contributor to the *Kitchen Explorers* blog on PBSparents.org, and often appears on television, radio, and in magazines such as *O, The Oprah Magazine, Real Simple, Working Mother, Kiwi, Every Day with Rachael Ray, Prevention*, and many others.

1. Cook the noodles according to the package directions until they are al dente. Drain and toss them immediately in a large bowl with 1 tbsp oil.

2. While the noodles are cooking, heat 1 tbsp oil over medium-high heat in a wok or large skillet (nonstick is best for tofu) and add the chicken (or tofu).

3. Cook, tossing often, until the chicken is no longer pink, about 3 minutes (or the tofu is lightly browned, about 5 minutes). Add the chicken (or tofu) to the bowl with the noodles.

4. Add the remaining 2 tbsp oil to the skillet over medium-high heat and add the peppers, carrots, onions, green onions, and red pepper flakes. Cook, stirring frequently, until the vegetables are crisp-tender, about 3 minutes.

5. Add the noodles, chicken (or tofu), soy sauce, and teriyaki or stir-fry sauce to the pan and toss together for 1 minute.

6. Serve hot or chill for up to 24 hours and serve it cold.

THAI CHICKEN NOODLE SOUP

You can substitute tofu for chicken in this dish sweetly flavored
with coconut milk and peanut butter

The Six O'Clock Scramble

www.thescramble.com

Chef Aviva Goldfarb

Serves 6

1 tbsp vegetable oil

1 tsp minced garlic (about 2 cloves)

1 lb/450 g boneless, skinless chicken breast or extra-firm tofu, cut into ½-in/1-cm pieces

¾ tsp turmeric

¼ tsp cayenne pepper (optional)

6 cups/1.5 L reduced-sodium chicken or vegetable broth

¾ cup/180 ml light, unsweetened coconut milk

3 tbsp fresh lime juice

3 tbsp smooth, natural peanut butter

2 cups/115 g thin egg noodles

1 tbsp sugar

2 tbsp fresh cilantro, chopped (optional)

1. In a large stockpot, heat the oil over medium heat. Add the garlic and stir-fry it for 1 minute until light golden in color and fragrant.

2. Add the chicken (or tofu), turmeric, and cayenne and stir-fry for 3-4 minutes, until the chicken is partially cooked.

3. Add the broth, coconut milk, lime juice, peanut butter, and noodles. Bring the soup to a low boil, partially cover the pot, and simmer the soup for 15 minutes. Stir in the sugar and cilantro, and serve hot.

Chef Aviva Goldfarb

Aviva Goldfarb is a family-dinner expert who helps busy parents let go of all the stress at 6:00 and bring joy and good nutrition back to the dinner table. She is a mother of two and the author and founder of The Six O'Clock Scramble, www.thescramble.com, an online dinner planning system and cookbook (St. Martin's Press, 2006), and is author of *SOS! The Six O'Clock Scramble to the Rescue: Earth Friendly, Kid-Pleasing Meals for Busy Families* (St. Martin's Press, 2010), which was named one of the best cookbooks of 2010 by *The Washington Post*. She is also a weekly contributor to the *Kitchen Explorers* blog on PBSparents.org, and often appears on television, radio, and in magazines such as *O, The Oprah Magazine, Real Simple, Working Mother, Kiwi, Every Day with Rachael Ray, Prevention*, and many others.

THAI LASAGNA

Homemade rice lasagna noodles are filled with a tropical mango
salad alternating with a cashew chicken layer

Hawaii Food Tours

www.HawaiiFoodTours.com

Chef Matthew Gray

Chef Matthew Gray

Gray, a former professional chef, has cooked for
movie stars and rock and roll bands. He was the
food writer and restaurant critic for Hawaii's
largest newspaper for several years before starting
Hawaii Food Tours, voted the best tour in
Hawaii for the past two years.

Serves 8-10

For Rice Noodles:

See page 26 or page 118 for a list of ingredients and step-by-step directions.

For Thai Fresh Mango Salad Layer:

2 fresh limes

1 tbsp naturally-fermented soy sauce

1 tbsp honey

1 tbsp granulated sugar

1 small serrano pepper, seeded and minced or ½ tsp hot red chili
    flakes

2 tbsp peanut oil

Salt to taste

3-4 ripe firm, fragrant mangoes, any variety will suffice (or 6 large, fra-
    grant peaches), sliced and then chopped into pieces

2 sweet bell peppers, preferably 1 red and 1 yellow, cut in very thin strips

1 large (or 2 medium) carrots, coarsely grated

2 green onions, thinly sliced

½ cup/16 g roughly chopped fresh cilantro

½ cup/35 g roughly chopped mint

3 cups/265 g romaine lettuce, ribs removed, torn into bite-size pieces

1 cup/115 g chopped, oven-toasted walnuts or pecans

1. Grate the peel from 1 lime
   and place into a non-metallic
   bowl. Add ½ cup lime juice.
   Then whisk in soy sauce,
   honey, sugar, and serrano
   pepper until the sugar is
   completely dissolved. Slowly
   whisk in peanut oil until
   combined (emulsified) fully.
   Add salt, if necessary, to taste,
   and set dressing aside.

2. Mix mangoes, peppers,
   carrots, and green onions with
   cilantro and mint.

3. Add lettuce and toss gently
   until combined.

4. Place lettuce and mango
   mixture in a large bowl. Toss
   with dressing until mixed.
   Add toasted walnuts or pecans
   and mix.

For Grilled Chicken with
    Cashew Satay Sauce Layer:

For the Marinade:

4 cloves garlic, sliced

3 shallots, sliced

3 tbsp brown sugar

3 tbsp fresh lime juice

3 tbsp peanut or canola oil

1½ tbsp chili garlic paste

1 tbsp orange zest, chopped finely

1 tbsp lime zest, chopped finely

1 tbsp grated fresh ginger

1 tbsp ground coriander

1 tbsp ground turmeric

½ cup/120 ml coconut milk

2 lb/900 g chicken breasts or chicken
    "tenders," cut into bite-sized pieces,
    sprinkled with salt and pepper

1. Puree or process all marinade
   ingredients.

2. Combine chicken with marinade,
   stirring well, then cover and place
   in refrigerator 1-24 hours in
   advance.

For Cashew Satay Sauce:

½ cup/120 ml water

½ cup/120 ml coconut milk

½ cup/115 g cashew butter (process your cashews, or buy at
    store)

2 tbsp brown sugar

1 tbsp chili garlic paste

1 tbsp naturally-fermented soy sauce

1 tbsp canola oil

¼ cup/30 g chopped cashews

1 tbsp minced garlic

1 tsp curry powder

2 tsp grated fresh ginger

1 tbsp fresh lime juice

1. Make cashew satay sauce: Combine water, coconut milk,
   cashew butter, brown sugar, chili garlic paste, and soy
   sauce; set aside.

2. Heat oil in a small saucepan over low-medium heat. Add
   cashews, garlic, curry powder, and ginger, stirring until
   fragrant, about 2 minutes.

3. Whisk in coconut milk, mix, and simmer 5 minutes. Stir in
   lime juice, and set sauce aside.

4. Preheat large sauté pan.

5. Put a little oil into pan. Place chicken pieces in the pan in
   one layer (do not crowd pan), and brown 2-3 minutes on
   each side. Do in multiple batches if necessary.

6. Combine browned chicken pieces with cashew satay sauce.

To assemble: Place one lasagna noodle in a deep, round metal
or ceramic dish. Add a layer of Grilled Chicken with Cashew
Satay Sauce, then another noodle and a layer of Thai Fresh
Mango Salad. Continue alternating noodles and fillings, until
both are all used.

Serve immediately.

THAI SESAME NOODLES

Wheat noodles with chicken and sesame seeds get a
flavor boost from shrimp paste and fish sauce

LAGUNA PHUKET
RESORT AND VILLAS

Panache

142/3 Moo 6, Laguna Village
Cherngtalay, Phuket 83110,
Thailand
66 76 336 900

Cuisine: Thai

Chef Robert Czeschka

At Panache Restaurant, guests experience
poolside, al fresco, and indoor dining with a
spectacular interactive kitchen concept. The
International and Asian cuisine emphasizes
casual, creative, and healthy preparations
and offers a delightful spin on made-to-
order meals where chefs prepare dishes to a
customer's particular preference.

Serves 4-6

For the Marinade:

3 tbsp soy sauce

2 tbsp sesame oil

1 tbsp rice vinegar

¾ tsp sugar

2 boneless chicken breasts, cut into strips

12 oz/340 g dried wheat noodles

3-4 tbsp sesame seeds

Vegetable oil, for stir-frying

1 thumb-size piece ginger, grated or finely chopped

3 cloves garlic, minced

1 red bell pepper

5-8 mushrooms

For the Sauce:

¼ cup/60 ml fresh-squeezed lime juice

2 tbsp soy sauce

1 tbsp sesame oil

1 tbsp fish sauce

½ tsp shrimp paste

2-3 tsp sugar, to taste

1 fresh red chili, minced or ½ tsp dried crushed chili
   flakes

Garnishes:

1-2 green onions (the green part sliced), a handful
   fresh basil, lime wedges, Thai chili sauce

Chef Robert Czeschka

Chef Czescha is an Austrian national with twenty-six years of experience, including sixteen years as an Executive Chef in Germany, Egypt, Malaysia, Thailand, China, and most recently at the luxury Nam Hai Resort in Hoi An, Vietnam.

1. Stir together marinade ingredients and pour over chicken strips in a bowl. Allow to marinate in the refrigerator while preparing other ingredients.

2. Stir together all sauce ingredients with a fork or whisk in a small bowl until shrimp paste and sugar dissolve; set aside.

3. Boil noodles until "al dente." Rinse thoroughly with cold water to keep from sticking, and set aside.

4. Place sesame seeds in a dry frying pan over medium heat. Stir until seeds turn light golden brown. Transfer to a bowl to cool.

5. Heat a wok or large frying pan over medium heat and drizzle 1-2 tbsp oil into pan. Add the ginger and garlic. Stir-fry for 1 minute, then add the chicken including the marinade. Stir-fry 3 minutes or till chicken is cooked through.

6. Add the red pepper and mushrooms, stir-fry 1 more minute or until mushrooms are cooked.

7. Add noodles and then pour in the sauce. Stir-fry for another 1 minute using a tossing motion.

8. Remove from heat, sprinkle two-thirds of the toasted sesame seeds on the noodles and toss again, seasoning with salt and spice. If too salty for your taste, you may add another tbsp lime juice; if not salty or flavorful enough, add a sprinkling of fish sauce. You can also add additional chili for more heat.

9. To serve, put noodles on individual serving plates, adding a final sprinkling of sesame seeds to each portion. Top with greens of the green onion, fresh basil and lime wedges. Serve Thai chili sauce on the side for those who like it spicy.

VIETNAMESE CHICKEN PHO NOODLE SOUP

Herbs and spices and chicken in a flavorful broth

BT

EAT LOCAL - THINK GLOBAL

BT

2507 South MacDill Avenue #B
Tampa, FL 33629
(813) 258-1916

Cuisine: French-Vietnamese

Chef BT Nguyen

BT is a gourmet restaurant with an international flavor, most notably its distinctive French-Vietnamese hybrid dishes.

Chef BT Nguyen

BT's obsession with the kitchen began as a child in Vietnam. At the fall of Saigon, a young BT began a long journey finally ending in the United States. After college, she continued her passion for cooking while pursuing a career in the fashion industry. Ultimately, BT left the fashion industry to become a restaurateur.

Serves 6-8

For the Broth:

2 yellow onions, cut in half

2 oz/60 g fresh ginger, crushed

3 sticks cinnamon

2 tbsp coriander seeds

1 tbsp peppercorns

10 star anise

1 tbsp cardamom

2 2½ lb/1 kg whole organic chickens

3 lb/1.5 kg organic chicken bones

2 carrots

½ bunch of celery

2 daikon radishes

¼ head of green cabbage

6 qt/6 L filtered water

3½ tbsp fish sauce (best quality, low-sodium)

1 oz/28 g rock sugar

1. Place the onions and ginger directly on a medium-hot grill. Using tongs, rotate onion and ginger occasionally, cooking until slightly soft. Set aside.

2. Put cinnamon sticks, coriander seeds, peppercorns, star anise, and cardamom in a dry skillet and toast for five minutes to release the oil.

3. To achieve a clear broth, put both chicken and bones in a 10 quart soup pot. Fill water to cover the chicken. Bring to a boil over high heat; let it boil vigorously for 3 minutes to release the impurities. Pour the chicken and water into a clean sink, and then rinse the chicken and bones with cold water to wash off all residue.

4. Clean out the same pot and return the chicken and bones into the pot with grilled onions, ginger, all toasted spices, and vegetables.

5. Pour in the water. Bring to a boil over high heat and then lower the heat to simmer. Use a ladle to skim off any scum that rises to the top. Simmer for 45 minutes.

6. Remove the four chicken breasts and set aside. Continue simmering broth for one and a half hours.

7. Strain the broth through a fine mesh sieve. Add fish sauce and sugar, adjusting to suit your taste.

---

1 lb/450 g fresh noodles

1 lb/450 g bean sprouts

Shreddred cooked chicken breasts (from above)

12 sprigs of Thai basil

12 fresh cilantro leaves

3 Thai chilies, thinly sliced

1 red onion, sliced paper thin

1 cup/60 g green onions, chopped

1 cup/32 g chopped cilantro

1 cup/160 g roasted shallots (can be bought in any Asian market)

Black pepper to taste

2 limes, cut into wedges

Hot sauce

Hoisin sauce

1. Place fresh noodles in a colander or strainer and dip in boiling water for 30 seconds. Drain well.

2. Untangle noodles and divide into eight portions.

3. In each of eight bowls, place bean sprouts, noodles, chicken breast, basil, all of the cilantro, chilies, onions, green onions, shallots, and pepper.

4. Pour hot broth on top.

5. Add lime juice, hot sauce, and hoisin sauce to taste.

VIETNAMESE CHICKEN AND GINGER NOODLE SOUP

Soup for a crowd with an abundance of flavors

butterfly
San Francisco - Embarcadero

Butterfly

Alcatrez Ferries, Pier 33
The Embarcadero
San Francisco, CA 94133
(415) 864-8999

Cuisine: Eclectic

Chef Rob Lam

The floor-to-ceiling windows at Butterfly offer dramatic views of San Francisco's bay. Robert Lam is committed to supporting San Francisco's diverse and innovative artistic communities. As part of his commitment, works by local artists adorn the walls of Butterfly.

Serves 15

For Chicken Stock:

4 shallots

3 onions, halved

½ lb/230 g ginger, whole

15 lb/7 kg organic chicken bones

5 gal/2 dcl water

2 cinnamon sticks

2 cloves

2 star anise

8 black peppercorns

8 white peppercorns

8 coriander seeds

8 garlic cloves, peeled

2 cups/475 ml fish sauce

1 bunch parsley

4 bay leaves

4 carrots, peeled, and rough chopped

1 bunch celery, rough chopped, no leaves

4 onions, peeled, rough chopped

3 2 lb/900 g whole chickens, brined

1. Brûlée the shallots, onion, and ginger by placing cut halves onto a skillet or sauté pan and cooking until burnt.

2. Place them and all remaining ingredients except the carrots, celery and onion (mirepoix), and chickens in a large stockpot and bring to a boil.

3. Once boiling, immediately pull off to the side of the burners and skim. Then add the mirepoix. Lower heat and simmer for 1 hour.

4. Add the chickens and poach till done. (We prefer to brine our chickens before we poach them. Typical brines are 60% salt and 40% water with aromatics like garlic, bay leaf, peppercorns, thyme, pepper flakes. Brine/marinate the chicken for 2 hours and then poach in the stock till done.)

5. Chill, then shred the chickens and save for later. Strain the stock through a fine chinoise and chill immediately in preparation for the addition of the consommé raft.

For Consommé Raft:

3 gal/1dcl chicken stock

3 lb/1.3 kg chicken, thigh and breast meat, ground

2 tbsp each garlic and ginger, peeled and minced

¼ bunch cilantro, chopped

¼ bunch green onions, chopped

2 tomatoes, rough chopped

½ lemon, juiced

3 tbsp oyster sauce

3 tbsp soy sauce

½ cup/120 ml fish sauce

14 egg whites

32 oz/1 kg dried pho rice noodles

Garnish: Bean sprouts, cilantro leaf, basil leaf, jalapeño, hoisin sauce, and garlic chili sauce

Chef Rob Lam

Robert Lam, named one of six "Rising Star Chefs" by the *San Francisco Chronicle*, was born in Vietnam and calls his cooking "Asian within Asian," pulling from culinary traditions from Vietnamese, Thai, Chinese, Japanese, and Korean. He is a graduate of the Culinary Institute of America.

1. Pour chilled chicken stock in a large stockpot.

2. Combine ground chicken with all ingredients and mix thoroughly, making sure that the egg whites are evenly dispersed through the mix.

3. Add to the stock and put on a medium-high heat. It is very important that you stir frequently from this point on. Stir and scrape from the bottom of the pot for as long as it takes for the stock to reach bath water temperature. Stir every 2-4 minutes.

4. Once the "raft" has started to form (when you can see the egg whites starting to cook and form a round stage on top of the pot), stop stirring and pull the pot off to the side of the burners (or turn heat to very low). This will prevent too much direct heat from getting underneath the stock, and allow it to simmer without burning the bottom. Simmer for up to another hour once the raft is formed. Strain the stock by gently discarding the raft with a large slotted kitchen spoon or a large iron mesh skimmer and then pouring the stock thru a coffee filter or chinois. Adjust the seasoning and chill if not serving immediately.

5. Cook the noodles according to the package directions, and drain.

6. To serve: Place the cooked chicken meat over boiled noodles, pour hot broth over the top and garnish with bean sprouts, cilantro leaf, basil leaf, jalapeño, hoisin sauce, and garlic chili sauce.

YUZU CHICKEN AND MUSHROOM RAMEN

A long, slow simmer results in a richly flavored soup

Jin Ramen

3183 Broadway
New York, NY 10027
(646) 559-2862

Cuisine: Japanese

Chef Richard Kashida

Jin is the Japanese pronunciation of the character 仁. It means "benevolence" and finds its root in Confucian ideals. The character Jin consists of two elements. The left side represents a human being and the right side represents the numeral two. Jin is said to depict the way two people should treat one another. The founding partners of Jin Ramen chose Jin as their ramen bar's name not only out of an enthusiasm for ramen, but also from a desire to grow a business that has a positive impact on their Harlem community.

Serves 4

For the Stock:

Whole chicken, 3-4 lb/1.5-2 kg

1 gal/4 L water

½ lb/230 g shiitake mushrooms, stems for stock, tops for topping

2 lb/900 g bok choy, stems and trimmings for stock, tops and leaves for toppings

1 large Spanish onion, diced

2 carrots, diced

1 head cabbage, finely chopped

3 stalks celery, diced

½ lb/230 g kelp (seaweed)

2 bunches green onions, green ends only

For the Toppings:

Chicken breasts and dark meat from whole chicken, above, marinated in 2 tbsp soy sauce, 1 tbsp rice vinegar, salt, pepper and 1 tsp yuzu kosho

Tops and leaves from bok choy, above, julienned

1 package enoki mushrooms

Tops of shiitake mushrooms from above, julienned

1 tbsp butter

Salt and pepper, to taste

2 packages of dried ramen noodles, fresh is preferred if available

½ tsp yuzu kosho

½ lb/30 g bean sprouts

White ends of green onions, from above, julienned

For Tare Base:

2 tbsp salt

2 tbsp rice vinegar

4 tbsp mirin

1 tbsp soy sauce

1. Remove the breast and dark meat from the chicken and marinate as directed (see For the Toppings, left). Wash the rest of the chicken and place into a pot with enough cold water to cover.

2. Bring water to a boil. This will be your first wash. Let chicken bones boil for 15 minutes. Remove bones and dump water. Rinse the bones to clean off any additional impurities.

3. Fill a stockpot with the 1 gal/4 L of water and bring to a boil. Add the washed bones to the stockpot and return to a boil again. Then lower heat to a simmer.

4. Add mushroom stems, bok choy stems and leaf trimmings, and remaining stock ingredients to the pot.

5. Cook for another 2½ hours. Then strain out all vegetables, and chicken bones. Continue to simmer over low heat, skimming any remaining fat or impurities, while preparing toppings.

6. Mix all Tare Base ingredients together.

7. Sauté, grill, or broil the marinated chicken.

8. Steam the already cleaned bok choy.

9. Sauté the julienned Shiitake and Enoki mushrooms with 1 tbsp butter until brown and season with salt and pepper.

10. Cook noodles according to package directions.

11. Divide tare base evenly between 4 serving bowls.

12. Add 1/8 tsp yuzu kosho and 16 oz/475 ml hot broth to each bowl.

13. Add cooked noodles to broth and mix them so they don't stick together.

14. Top with the sliced chicken, bok choy, mushrooms, bean sprouts, and white parts of green onions.

VEGETABLE

BANGKOK-STYLE PAD THAI

A sweet and salty noodle dish

Khao San Road

326 Adelaide Street West
Toronto ON M5V 1R3
Canada
(647) 352-5773

Cuisine: Thai

Chef Chantana "Top" Chapman

Khao San Road is a massively
popular casual restaurant serving
Thai food in the heart of Toronto.
It has an abundance of appreciative
fans. From the start, its approach
has been simple: a short menu,
affordable prices, and a happy team
with no attitude.

Serves 3-4

For Pad Thai Sauce:

1 cup/240 ml tamarind juice

1⅓ cup/265 g coconut sugar

½ cup/120 ml plus 1 tbsp fish sauce

Mix all ingredients in a bowl, stirring until sugar dissolves. Taste and adjust ingredients to suit your preference.

Chef Chantana "Top" Chapman

Growing up in Bangkok, Thailand, Chef Chantana "Top" Chapman's mother taught her to appreciate and love food from a young age. Later she would study culinary arts in her home city, before coming to Canada in 2008. As a certified Thai Chef, she brings vast knowledge and skills, ranging across the culinary landscape of Thailand with a focus on Bangkok and central style street food, to Khao San Road.

Some of Chef Top's other passions include dancing; the love of her community, both Toronto and Thailand; animal welfare, pariculary the majestic elephants of Thailand; and, of course, her daughter.

2½ tbsp cooking oil

2 tbsp cut pressed tofu, cut in slivers

1 tbsp dried shrimp

1 tbsp shallot, minced

2 tbsp pickled radish, chopped

⅓ lb/150 g rice noodle

½ cup/120 ml water

¼ cup/60 ml pad thai sauce (left)

1 large egg

1 cup/100 g bean sprouts

¼ cup/12 g chives, cut in 1 in/2.5 cm pieces

2 tbsp crushed roasted peanuts

1. Heat 1 tbsp oil in a wok over medium heat. When oil is hot, add tofu and fry until lightly browned. Remove from wok and set aside.

2. Add dried shrimp to the wok and fry until crispy. Set aside.

3. Heat remaining oil in the wok over medium heat. When hot, add shallot; fry until fragrant. 4. Add fried tofu, pickled radish and fried shrimp. Stir for a few minutes.

4. Add noodles, water and pad thai sauce. Stir until the sauce cover all noodles.

5. Make room for egg in the middle. Scramble with spatula, and spread egg in a thin layer.

6. When set, mix together with other ingredients.

7. Add bean sprouts, and chives. Mix all ingredients thoroughly. Taste and adjust seasoning.

8. Spoon onto a serving plate, sprinkle with peanuts, and serve hot.

BREAKFAST CHEE CHEONG FUN

Noodles for breakfast using your microwave—sort of like Asian pancakes

Lily's Wai Sek Hong

Chef Lily Ng

www.lilyng2000.blogspot.com

Lily's Wai Sek Hong is a popular food blog administered by Lily Ng, a stay-at-home grandmother in Aurora, Colorado, who taught herself to cook and bake from cookbooks and by watching cooking programs on television.

Serves 3

For the Sauce:

½ cup/120 ml hoisin sauce

¼ cup/50 g sugar

2 tbsp sesame paste

2 tbsp soy sauce

1 cup/240 ml water

Mix all the ingredients together and cook in the microwave for 2 minutes until sugar is dissolved and sesame paste is well combined.

For the Chee Cheong Fun Batter:

1 cup/150 g cooked rice

3 cups/700 ml water

1 cup/150 g rice flour

¼ cup/23 g cake flour

3 tbsp tapioca starch

½ tsp salt

1 tbsp cooking oil

Additional oil for brushing

Garnish:

Roasted sesame seeds

Fried shallots

Follow the step-by-step instructions on page 188 to microwave the batter to make chee cheong fun.

1. Puree the rice with 2 cups/475 ml water until liquified.

2. Mix the remaining 1 cup/240 ml water with rice flour, cake flour, tapioca starch, and salt until well combined.

3. Add this to the liquified rice batter and blend well.

4. Pass this blended batter through a fine sieve and leave overnight in the fridge. (I have used the batter straight without resting and it made good chee cheong fun but resting made better ones.)

5. When ready to use, stir in the oil.

About Hoisin Sauce

This is a most misunderstood condiment. The word, hoisin, comes from a Romanization of the Chinese word for seafood. However, it does not contain seafood and it is not usually used with seafood. Its other common name is Plum Sauce, but it does not have any plums in it either! Hoisin sauce is usually made with mashed roasted soy beans, some kind of starch (usually rice, sweet potato, or rice), sugar, vinegar, and seasonings like red chili peppers, garlic, salt, and sesame seeds. It is most commonly used in soups and in dipping sauces and glazes.

BREAKFAST CHEE CHEONG FUN

continued

1. Use a microwavable plastic container with a very flat base. This one is 8 inch x 9 inch (20 cm x 22.5 cm).

2. Grease the base of plastic container.

3. Stir the batter very well and use a ladle to scoop up ½ cup/120 ml. Remember to stir every time you scoop the batter to make the next piece of chee cheong fun.

4. Pour batter into greased plastic container.

5. Tilt the plastic container until the base is covered with batter.

6. ½ cup/120 ml of batter is jut the right amount to cover the base of this plastic container.

7. Cover the filled plastic container with cling wrap and cook in the microwave on high for 2 minutes.

8. Remove plastic container from microwave and let it sit for 5 minutes before removing the cling wrap. Be very careful when you remove the cling wrap. Remove the cling wrap that is farthest away from you so that the steam will not burn you.

9. Brush the cooked chee cheong fun with oil.

How to Serve:

1. Cut up a few rolled-up chee cheong fun into bite-sized pieces and add in a couple of spoonfuls of the sauce (see page 186.)

2. Sprinkle with roasted sesame seeds and fried shallots. If you prefer something spicy, add in some chili sauce or, better still, some pickled green chilies or jalapeños. You can also drizzle a little of the oil used to fry the shallots on top, if you wish.

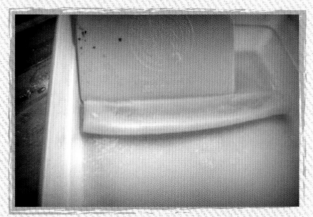

10. Using a bench scraper, scrape the chee cheong fun out of the plastic container. Chee cheong fun is ready to be enjoyed.

BUDDHIST RAMEN

Ten kinds of vegetables are used for the stock in this soup

Jin Ramen

3183 Broadway
New York, NY 10027
(646) 559-2862

Cuisine: Japanese

Chef Richard Kashida

Jin is the Japanese pronunciation of the character 仁. It means "benevolence" and finds its root in Confucian ideals. The character Jin consists of two elements. The left side represents a human being and the right side represents the numeral two. Jin is said to depict the way two people should treat one another. The founding partners of Jin Ramen chose Jin as their ramen bar's name not only out of an enthusiasm for ramen, but also from a desire to grow a business that has a positive impact on their Harlem community.

Serves 2

For Vegetarian Stock:

3 ears of corn, steamed and the kernels removed
        and set aside for a topping, below right;
        cobs go in stock

½ head cabbage

1 apple, cut in half and cored

1 piece ginger, split in half

1 bulb garlic, peeled and split in half

1 bunch green onions, green part only

1 potato, cut into quarters

7 oz/200 g egg shells

8 Japanese shiitake mushrooms, cut in half

1 sweet onion, cut in half

3½ oz/100 g kelp

2 carrots, chopped

½ head napa cabbage

For Dashi Broth (used in Tare):

3½ oz/100 g kombu

Boil 2 cups/475 ml water with kombu until
reduced down to 1 cup.

For Shio Tare:

2 oz/60 g salt

1 tsp mirin

1 tsp rice wine vinegar

1 tsp soy sauce

1 cup/240 ml dashi broth (below left)

Combine all ingredients and bring to a boil. Turn
        off and cool down.

⅓ lb/130 g fresh ramen noodles, cooked to desired
doneness

Toppings (use to your taste):

Shiitake mushrooms

Soft tofu, sliced

Green onions, white part thinly sliced

Bok choy, steamed

Corn, kernels from cobs used in stock (above left)

Yuzu koshyo (Ground Yuzu)

Enoki mushrooms

Shichimi togarashi (Japanese seven-spice powder)

Sesame seeds

For the Stock:

1. Wash and chop all stock ingredients and put in a large stockpot with 1 gal/4 L of water over high heat.

2. Once boiling, lower the heat to a simmer and reduce liquid down to about 1 qt/1.2 L (approximately 3 hours). Skim impurities throughout this process. Rule of thumb: Always start with three to four times more water than what you would like to end with.

3. Strain out vegetables from the broth.

Assembling the bowls:

1. Preheat 2 bowls. Mix ⅛ tsp of yuzu kosho, ⅛ cup/30 ml of tare and 16 oz/475 ml of hot broth into each bowl.

2. Mix in cooked noodles so they aren't stuck together.

3. Add toppings of your choice and/or additional seasoning.

BURMESE-STYLE NOODLE AND PAPAYA SALAD WITH TAMARIND DRESSING

The homemade tamarind dressing has a bit of kick

OUR CUISINE GETS PERSONAL

Chef Mya Zeronis

Mya Zeronis is the chef/owner of Lean Chef En Route, a personal chef and catering business in Pittsburgh, PA, and Zest Wishes, a health food and juice stand at the Pittsburgh Public Market. Prior to starting these ventures, she was executive chef at DC Bread and Brew, a green-certified, locally-sourced restaurant. Self-taught and competitive, she won top prizes in nine recipe contests within one year. Her grand-prize-winning recipe was published in *Taste of Home* magazine in October 2012.

Serves 2-4

¼ cup/60 ml peanut oil

4 cloves garlic, peeled and thinly sliced

1 pinch turmeric powder

1 (12-14oz/340-400 g) block non-GMO extra
    firm tofu, pressed to release excess water;
    cut in ½ in/1.25 cm cubes

1 lb/450 g fresh lo mein or soba noodles,
    cooked as instructed on package

1 green (about 1.5 lb/680 g) papaya, peeled,
    seeded, and shredded

2 medium shallots, thinly sliced

½ cup/80 g dry roasted peanuts, ground in a
    spice grinder or with a mortar and pestle
    until smooth

½ cup/15 g cilantro, roughly chopped

1 tsp chili pepper flakes, lightly toasted
    (for garnish)

Salt to taste

1. Heat oil in a skillet over low heat. Slowly
    fry garlic in oil until golden and crispy. Add
    turmeric. Remove garlic chips from pan;
    drain on paper towel.

2. Raise heat to medium-high. In remaining
    oil, sear tofu, stirring a few times, until
    golden brown. Transfer contents of skillet
    into a large mixing bowl.

3. Add all ingredients to the bowl, except
    garlic chips and pepper flakes, and
    mix with tamarind dressing (right).
    Sprinkle toasted pepper flakes and
    garlic chips on top.

Tamarind Dressing

1½ oz/40 g dried tamarind pulps

¾ cup/180 ml boiling water

1 tsp minced ginger

2 tbsp oyster sauce or tamari sauce

1 tbsp sriracha sauce

1. Make the dressing: Place tamarind pulps
    in a nonreactive bowl. Pour boiling hot
    water to cover them. Let tamarind soak in
    water for at least 5 minutes or until soft.

2. Wearing a glove, pulverize tamarind pulps
    by hand until they yield thick juice.
    Strain juice.

3. Whisk together with ginger, oyster sauce
    and sriracha sauce.

CHILI SATE NOODLES

Intense flavor comes from using raw peanuts and peanut sauce to make this dish

BaoQi

620 Davie Street
Vancouver, British Columbia
V6B5B6, Canada
(604) 700-4100

Cuisine: Vietnamese

Chef Kim Dieu Tran

Vietnamese comfort food is the fare at this family-owned and family-run restaurant featuring fresh ingredients and a pleasant dining experience.

Serves 4-5

8 oz/200g raw peanuts, dry roasted, ground
    moderately fine

10 stalks lemongrass, tender inner part, finely
    minced

1½ tbsp dried ground chilies

1 tbsp fresh ground chilies

32 oz/950 ml vegetable stock

1 cup/240 ml thick, sweet black bean sauce (or
    peanut sauce)

4 shallots, minced

4 cloves garlic, minced

2 tbsp palm oil

2 tbsp tamarind juice (soak tamarind in hot
    water, squeeze, and strain to obtain juice)

1 cup/240 ml coconut milk

2 tbsp palm sugar

2 tsp sea salt

8 oz/200 g cooked rice or egg noodles

Garnishes:

Ground peanuts

Cilantro

Bean sprouts

Tomatoes

Basil

Lime wedges

Pickled vegetables

1. Combine all ingredients except noodles
   in a large pot and stir until well blended.
   Cook over medium heat until peanuts
   are soft, adding more vegetable stock as
   needed if the sauce gets too thick.

2. Ladle sate sauce over noodles, garnish as
   desired and serve.

Chef Kim Dieu Tran

Kim Dieu Tran worked at the U.S. Embassy in
Saigon until it fell to the North Vietnamese,
when she bought a boat and escaped from
Vietnam to Thailand, losing almost everything
to pirates along the way. She and her husband
arrived in Canada in 1979 as refugees.

About Lemongrass

Lemongrass is a common ingredient of Thai,
Vietnamese, and other Asian recipes. Known
for its zesty lemon flavor and aroma, this herb is
used in recipes grated, minced, and sometimes
bruised and left whole to flavor soups or stews.
Lemongrass can be found fresh—its foot-long
stalks should be firm and not rubbery, with
a lower half that's pale yellow/white and an
upper half that's completely green. It can also
be purchased frozen, already grated and ready
to use.

CHINESE NOODLES

Vegetables and noodles—simple to make, simply delicious to eat

Show Me The Curry

www.showmethecurry.com

About the chefs

Showmethecurry.com is a website featuring step-by-step, easy-to-follow recipe videos that showcase South Asian cuisine. Hosted by Anuja and Hetal, two foodies and entrepreneurs, it has established a loyal following worldwide among people interested in a modern approach to traditional Indian cuisine.

Serves 6–8

16 oz/450 g egg noodles

1 tbsp sesame oil

2 tbsp oil

1 tbsp garlic, minced

1 tbsp ginger, minced

1 small onion, sliced

1 large carrot, cut into matchsticks

1½ cups/510 g cabbage, shredded

½ large bell pepper, cut into strips

8 baby corn, cut in half

1 egg (optional)

½ tsp black pepper or to taste

2 tbsp soy sauce or to taste

1 tbsp white vinegar

Hosin or any Chinese sauce, to taste

Red chili sauce (sambal), to taste

2 green onions, stalks cut diagonally – for garnish

About Ginger

This distinctive spice is used both fresh and in powder form to add zing and flavor. In addition to great taste, ginger claims important medicinal qualities. Although evidence is not conclusive, it is thought to be helpful in treating gastrointestinal disorders, especially nausea, and is often suggested as a remedy for morning sickness during pregnancy. Recent research points to the possibility of using compounds found in ginger to treat certain kinds of cancer in the future.

1. Cook noodles per package instructions (usually 3-4 minutes). Drain, rinse with cold water, and toss with sesame oil. Set aside.

2. Heat oil in a large wok-style pan over high heat.

3. Add garlic and ginger and cook for 30 seconds.

4. Add onions and cook for 30 seconds.

5. Add carrots and allow them to soften just a little.

6. Add cabbage, bell pepper, and baby corn. Toss well and cook for 1 minute.

7. Push veggies to one side of wok and break an egg in the pan.

8. Scramble the egg until cooked and mix together with the veggies.

9. Add black pepper and mix.

10. Toss noodles once before adding them to the pan.

11. Add soy sauce, white vinegar, hoisin sauce, and red chili sauce. Mix well to coat all noodles.

12. Taste and adjust any of the sauces to suit your taste.

13. Garnish with green onions and serve hot.

COCO-NOODLE-DOO SOUP

Lime juice and lots of cilantro gives this vegetable soup a fresh flavor

Serves 8

½ lb/230 g snow peas

1 8-oz/230-g can baby corn

1 bell pepper, any color

2 tbsp vegetable oil

1 medium yellow onion, diced

2 cloves garlic, minced

1 in/2½ cm piece fresh ginger, peeled and minced

32 oz/950 ml chicken or vegetable broth

8 oz/230 g vermicelli rice noodles

1 13 oz/390-ml can of coconut milk

4 limes, juiced

1 cup/32 g fresh cilantro leaves, chopped

1 bunch of green onions

Salt and pepper, to taste

1. Chop snow peas, baby corn, and bell pepper into ½ in/1 cm pieces and set aside.

2. In a large stockpot heat vegetable oil over medium heat. Add onion and cook while stirring constantly for about 2 minutes. Add garlic and ginger and continue to cook for about 3 minutes, stirring throughout.

3. Add chopped vegetables, stir, and continue to cook an additional 2 minutes.

4. Add broth and bring to a boil.

5. Add rice noodles to pot and bring back to a boil.

6. Lower to medium-low heat, cover, and simmer for 10 minutes.

7. Uncover and stir in coconut milk, lime juice, cilantro, green onions, salt, and pepper. Simmer for an additional 3-5 minutes.

The Creative Kitchen

www.thecreativekitchen.com

Chef Cricket Azima

Chef Cricket Azima

Cricket Azima, the founder of The Creative Kitchen, specializes in cooking for and with children. She consults with major food companies to develop recipes and blogs, and to create cooking webisodes. She also teaches cooking classes in New York City at schools, in specialty food stores, and in privately held classes. She has a masters degree in Food Studies and Food Management from New York University.

About Cilantro

This herb is so often found in Asian cuisine that it is sometimes called "Chinese Parsley." It comes from the coriander plant and in fact, fresh coriander and cilantro are one and the same. With a distinctive and sharper flavor than parsley, cilantro leaves and stems are used fresh in salads and as a garnish, and are also chopped and cooked in sauces, dressings, soups, and noodle dishes.

COLD SESAME NOODLES

The peanut flavor is nicely balanced with some additional vegetables in this
Chinese classic gourmet Asian street food

Mira Sushi & Izakaya

46 W. 22nd Street
New York, NY 10010
(212) 989-7889

Cuisine: Gourmet Asian Street Food

Chef Brian Tsao

This recently opened Flatiron-district
restaurant is overseen by Chef Brian,
along with sushi chef Owen Wu.

Serves 4

For the Sweet Soy Base:

¼ cup/60 ml soy sauce

¼ cup/60 ml water

¼ cup/60 ml white vinegar

¼ cup/50 g sugar

4 tbsp garlic, mashed to a paste

For the Sesame Sauce:

2 cups/475 ml Chinese sesame paste

3 tbsp sesame oil

1 cup/240 ml water

¼ cup/60 ml soy sauce

For the Noodles:

1 large cucumber, julienned

½ medium carrot, julienned

⅓ cup/80 ml vegetable oil

Salt to taste

1 ½ lb/675 g fresh Chinese thick egg noodles

½ cup/80 g unsalted roasted peanuts, finely
    ground

½ bunch green onions, green section only,
    chopped finely for garnish

1. In a container, combine all the ingredients
    for the sweet soy base the night before to
    allow the garlic to infuse the base.

2. Mix together all sesame sauce ingredients.

3. In a bowl, combine the julienned cucumber
    and carrot with oil and season lightly with
    salt. Reserve.

4. Cook noodles in a large pot of boiling water
    (water MUST be boiling). To check if the
    noodles are done, pull a piece and break it,
    if the center has a very small center of raw
    dough, it will need another minute. Once
    the noodles are done, immediately rinse in
    cold water, the colder the better!

5. Split the noodles between four bowls. Stir
    the soy base well and pour 3 tbsp over each
    noodle serving. Add ¼ cup sesame sauce
    and some ground peanuts.

6. Top with cucumber and carrot salad,
    garnish with green onions, and enjoy!

Chef Brian Tsao

Tsao, formerly of Telepan, comes from a
Chinese-Korean background. His wife is
Malaysian, and all of these different influences
are reflected in the foods he prepares. Before
graduating from the Culinary Institute of
America, Tsao was a musician and traveled
throughout Asia exploring different cuisines.

DOTORI KUKSU

Fresh acorn noodles

Contemporary Korean Kitchen

Contemporary Korean Kitchen offers cooking classes in New York City dedicated exclusively to the fine art of Korean cuisine. In Korean life and culture, food is not just for satisfying hunger and sustaining life. It is a celebration of life. H & Y Marketplace (www.hanyangmart.com) is a sponsor, providing ingredients for many of the cooking classes hosted by Contemporary Korean Kitchens, including the classes at which the recipes in this book were prepared.

Serves 2

For the Acorn Noodles:
1 oz/20 g acorn powder
2 oz/50 g organic wheat flour
1 tsp canola oil
4 tsp water
Salt

For the Sauce:
2 tsp Korean soy sauce (Joseon ganjang)
1 tsp brown rice vinegar
½ tsp sesame oil
½ tsp red pepper powder

For the Vegetables:
Water dropwort
Crown daisy
Red pepper

1. Mix acorn powder and flour and put it through a fine sieve.

2. Add canola oil, water, and salt to the dry ingredients and mix well to form a pasta dough. Cover it with plastic wrap and let it rest for at least 1½ hours.

3. Combine Korean soy sauce, brown rice vinegar, sesame oil, and red pepper powder in a bowl and mix well.

4. Gently tear water dropwort and crown daisy into bite size pieces. Julienne the red pepper and set aside.

5. Take the rested dough and roll it out in a pasta machine. Use the fettuccine attachment to cut your noodles. (If you do not have a pasta machine, you can roll it out and use a knife to cut the noodles.)

6. Bring a pot of salted water to a boil. Add noodles and cook for 3 minutes. Drain and quickly rinse in cold water.

7. To assemble: In a big bowl, add the prepared vegetables and dress them with the sauce, tossing with your hands. Add the cooked noodles and gently mix with the vegetables.

Chef Tony Yoo

Yoo apprenticed in restaurants throughout South Korea before venturing into Japan, Australia, America, and Europe. During the London Olympics, he served as an Executive Chef at the Embassy of the Republic of Korea in the United Kingdom, where he created and executed menus for gala dinners and other embassy functions. Yoo now works as a freelance chef and instructor for Contemporary Korean Kitchen.

FRIED SHIRATAKI NOODLES WITH BOK CHOY AND ROASTED SESAME SEEDS

Crunch and taste combine in this low-carb side dish

www.strictlypaleoish.com

The blog www.strictlypaleoish.com was started was started in early 2012 by a young dad in Sweden whose goal was to document what he cooked during his six-month paternity leave. While the blog does include occasional recipes with dairy, the majority of the recipes are strictly Paleo. Because of the fabulous response he has received from readers all over the world, he has continued updating the blog on weekends.

Serves 4

14 oz/400 g shirataki noodles (usually two bags)

½ cup/80 g sesame seeds

A few pinches of Chinese five-spice powder

2 tbsp coconut oil

1 tbsp tamari

2 heads bok choy, thinly shredded

1. Place the shirataki noodles in a colander and rinse thoroughly under running cold water, then let drain.

2. Roast the sesame seeds in a hot, dry frying pan until light brown, then pour them into a bowl and set aside.

3. Put the noodles in the still hot, dry frying pan and let most of the water evaporate. (I find this gives them a more pleasant texture.)

4. When most of water is evaporated, sprinkle a few pinches of five-spice over the noodles, add the coconut oil, and let fry for a minute or so while tossing to make sure the spices are evenly spread.

5. Add the tamari and roasted sesame seeds, then add the shredded bok choy.

6. Continue stir-frying and tossing so all components blend evenly and until the bok choy has softened.

About Bok Choy

This vegetable commonly used in southeast Asian cooking goes by a few names: pak choi, white vegetable, and white cabbage. It is classified as a cabbage, but with its small bulb at the bottom and leafy greens up top it doesn't resemble a cabbage. It has a light, sweet flavor, making it a favorite choice for soups, stir-fries, appetizers, and side and main dishes. An added bonus? It's high in calcium and Vitamins A and C but low in calories.

GLUTEN-FREE SPICY GINGER TOFU NOODLE SALAD

Red pepper flakes kick up the heat in this salad

Serves 4 as entrée, 6 as appetizer

⅓ cup/80 ml San-J Gluten Free Tamari
    Ginger Dressing

1 tsp garlic powder

½ tsp (more if you want it spicier)
    red pepper flakes

1 lb/450 g gluten-free brown rice fettuccini
    style pasta

1 lb/450 g firm tofu

Gluten-free nonstick cooking spray

4 oz/113 g shiitake mushrooms, stems removed,
    sliced

1 English cucumber

1 bunch cilantro, coarsely chopped

4 green onions, thinly sliced on the diagonal

1 red bell pepper, cut into small dice

Salt and pepper

1 tsp sesame seeds

Chef Carol Kicinski

Carol Kicinski is a professional recipe developer, television chef, magazine founder and editor-in-chief, freelance writer, and cookbook author—who cooks, writes, and travels, doing it all gluten-free! She prides herself in creating recipes that are not just "good for gluten-free," but just plain good! Her blog, simplygluten-free.com, is designed to share, teach, and inspire with gluten-free recipes.

1. Whisk together the San-J Gluten Free Tamari Ginger Dressing with the garlic powder and red pepper flakes.

2. Bring a large pot of salted water to a boil and cook the pasta according to the package directions. Drain and rinse with hot water. Add the dressing and toss to coat.

3. While the pasta is cooking, pat the tofu dry with paper towels and cut into 1 in/2.5 cm pieces. Heat a large skillet, heavily sprayed with nonstick cooking spray, over medium-high heat. Spray the pan heavily with nonstick cooking spray and add the tofu pieces. Let cook for 1–2 minutes undisturbed or until they are golden brown. Flip the pieces over and continue cooking until browned on all sides. When the tofu is done, remove from the skillet and add to the pasta.

4. Add the mushroom slices to the hot skillet and cook until browned, stirring often, about 2–3 minutes. Add the mushrooms to the pasta.

5. Peel the cucumber, cut in half lengthwise, scrape out the seeds, cut into thin slices and add to the pasta. Reserve some of the chopped cilantro for garnish, and add the rest to the pasta along with the green onions and bell pepper.

6. Toss everything together and season with salt and pepper to taste. Garnish with the reserved cilantro leaves and the sesame seeds.

About Gluten-free Noodles

It's hard to enjoy traditional noodle recipes if you're on a gluten-free diet. Fortunately there are gluten-free pastas. In addition to the one called for here made from brown rice, there are other varieties that use corn, a combination of corn and quinoa, potato, and soybeans in place of flour. The other potential gluten pitfall in Asian noodle recipes is in sauces and dressings, but modification or substitutions are usually available.

HONG KONG-STYLE CHOW MEIN NOODLES

Two kinds of chives and lots of bean sprouts give nice texture and balance to the other vegetables in this noodle dish

Oriental Garden

14 Elizabeth Street
New York, NY 10013
(212) 619-0085

Cuisine: Cantonese

Chef Wong

Located in the heart of Chinatown in New York City, Oriental Garden is known for its phenomenally fresh seafood, with crabs, fish, and lobster cooked fresh from its fish tanks. Cantonese in style, the restaurant frequently finds itself on lists for the best Chinese food in New York, with a wide range of hearty dim sum, stir-fried meats, and vibrant vegetable and tofu dishes, making the restaurant a perennial chef favorite.

Serves 2

4 oz/113 g bean sprouts

4 oz/113 g yellow chives

2 oz/56 g green chives

2 oz/56 g carrot

4 oz/113 g green onions

2 oz/56 g celery

2 oz/56 g snow pea pods

4 oz/113 g black mushrooms

½ cup/120 ml soya bean salad oil

8 oz/230 g chow mein noodles (can substitute yellow egg noodles)

½ tsp salt

2 tsp oyster sauce

2 tsp dark soy sauce

1 cup/240 ml water

1. Wash all vegetables and prepare them:

    Take the ends off the bean sprouts.

    Cut the yellow chives and green chives into 2 in/5 cm pieces.

    Slice the carrots, green onions, celery, snow pea pods, and black mushrooms into thin strips.

2. Heat the soya bean salad oil in a large wok.

3. Stir fry chow mein noodles until yellow and crispy all around. Remove from wok with slotted spoon and set aside (leaving the oil in the wok).

4. Add mushrooms, snow pea pods, carrots, celery, and green chives, along with salt, oyster sauce, and soy sauce.

5. Return noodles to wok with 1 cup of water and sauté until dry.

6. Add the bean sprouts and yellow chives, sauté briefly, and serve.

Chef Wong

Chef Wong started his culinary career in the iconic banquet halls of Hong Kong thirty-five years ago. An immigrant to New York, he has been at Oriental Garden for twenty-nine years, where he has made a name for himself with his mastery of a diversity of Hong Kong-style dishes. The pride of the restaurant, he is beloved by customers for the rich aroma and flavor of his culinary creations—whether braised, stir-fried, grilled, or stewed.

About Stir-frying

Stir-frying is a quick and healthy way to prepare foods. Here are a few tips for best results:

- Stir frying is fast! Have everything cut up before you begin cooking.

- Cut foods in similar-size pieces to ensure even cooking of all ingredients.

- Keep moving. Stir-fry recipes usually call for high heat, so keep tossing and stirring your ingredients to prevent burning.

- Cook in batches: Do meats first and remove; then do vegetables, starting with the denser ones first. Add all together in the end and toss a few more times to mix and heat through.

- When adding a sauce, make a well in the center of the ingredients and add sauce there. Allowing it to sit for a few seconds will thicken the sauce; then toss through all the ingredients.

JAPANESE SOBA NOODLES WITH GARLIC AND MUSHROOMS

Soba noodles or whole wheat linguine can be used in this chicken dish

The Six O'Clock Scramble

www.thescramble.com

Chef Aviva Goldfarb

Serves 6

10 oz/280 g Japanese soba noodles (or use whole wheat linguine)

4 tsp vegetable oil

¼ cup/60 ml reduced-sodium soy sauce (use wheat/gluten-free if needed)

2 tbsp rice vinegar

2 tbsp sweet Asian chili sauce

1 tbsp toasted sesame oil

4 oz/113 g sliced oyster mushrooms or exotic mushroom blend

1½ tsp minced garlic, about 3 cloves

1 cup/70 g snow peas, sliced

4 green onions, thinly sliced

1. Cook the soba noodles according to the package directions. Drain, then, return them to the pot and toss with 1 tsp vegetable oil.

2. In a large measuring cup, combine the soy sauce, vinegar, chili sauce, and sesame oil.

3. In a large nonstick skillet, heat 1 tbsp vegetable oil. When oil is hot, add the mushrooms and sauté them for 4–5 minutes until they are tender and fragrant.

4. Add garlic and snow peas and sauté them for about 1 minute. Add soy sauce mixture and cook for about 30 seconds until it comes to a boil.

5. Pour the vegetables and sauce over the noodles, toss gently, and top with the green onions. Serve immediately or refrigerate for up to 2 days. Serve hot or cold.

Chef Aviva Goldfarb

Aviva Goldfarb is a family-dinner expert who helps busy parents let go of all the stress at 6:00 and bring joy and good nutrition back to the dinner table. She is a mother of two and the author and founder of The Six O'Clock Scramble, www.thescramble.com, an online dinner planning system. She has also published several cookbooks and is also a weekly contributor to the *Kitchen Explorers* blog on PBSparents.org. Goldfarb often appears on television and radio, and her recipes appear in a variety of women's magazines.

KHAO SHWE THOKE

A cool and refreshing summer noodle salad

Daw Yee Myanmar Café

111 N Rural Drive
Monterey Park, CA 91755
(626) 573-8080

Cuisine: Burmese

Chef Delyn Chow

The restaurant is named after Chow's mother, whose recipes make up Chow's menu. Work from local artists adorn the walls.

Serves 2

1 tbsp garlic oil, store bought (or make your
own: 1 cup oil; 5 cloves garlic, chopped;
pinch of tumeric)

1 tbsp tamarind juice or lime juice

1 tsp fish sauce

1 tsp dried shrimp powder

1 tsp roasted chili flakes

1 tsp roasted chick pea powder (key ingredient)

1 cup/120 g cooked round egg noodles (can
substitute spaghetti)

½ cup/170 g shredded cabbage

½ cup/50 g cooked bean sprouts

¼ cup/40 g sliced raw onion (optional)

Garnish: cilantro, hard-boiled egg slices, lime,
fried dry rice noodles

1. Whisk garlic oil, tamarind juice, fish
sauce, shrimp powder, chili flakes, and
chick pea powder in a small bowl.

2. Combine noodles with cabbage, bean
sprouts, and onion and toss with dressing.

3. Plate the salad and garnish with cilantro,
hard-boiled egg slices, lime wedges, and
fried dry rice noodles.

Chef Delyn Chow

Chow is a second-generation Burmese chef/
restauranteur.

Roasting Spices

Why bother? It's because heat releases oils
and aromatics in spices, giving them a deeper,
more intense flavor. Savory spices take on an
earthier, slightly nutty flavor. Sweet spices, like
cinnamon or ginger, will get mellower and
sweeter when roasted. Roasting spices is easy:
Place the spices in a heavy pan over medium
low heat. Stir gently until the spices become
very fragrant and slightly darker in color—it
only takes a few minutes and the flavor boost it
gives to the dish you're cooking is well worth it.

KONGGUKSU

Rice noodles with chilled homemade soy milk broth

Contemporary Korean Kitchen offers cooking classes in New York City dedicated exclusively to the fine art of Korean cuisine. In Korean life and culture, food is not just for satisfying hunger and sustaining life. It is a celebration of life. H & Y Marketplace (www.hanyangmart.com) is a sponsor, providing ingredients for many of the cooking classes hosted by Contemporary Korean Kitchens.

Serves 2

1 cup/200 g dried black soybeans

2 tbsp sesame seeds, toasted

1 tsp sea salt

3 cups/700 ml chilled spring water or
purified water

8 oz/230 g rice noodles

¼ cup/75 g cucumbers, julienned and
sliced tomato for garnish

1. Soak the soybeans in cold water
   overnight.

2. Next day, drain the soybeans. Put into
   a pot, cover with water, and boil for 15
   minutes.

3. Drain and add cold water. When you rub
   the beans with your fingers, the skin will
   come off. Once the skins are off, you can
   add more water and swirl them around
   and the skin will float to the top. Discard
   all skins.

4. Put the skinned soybeans in the blender
   with toasted sesame seeds, salt, and
   spring water. Blend until smooth. It will
   look like frothy milk. Keep the soymilk
   in the refrigerator until the noodles are
   done.

5. Cook the noodles according to the
   package instructions. After the noodles
   are done, drain and rinse in cold water
   several times.

6. To serve, mound the noodles in a bowl
   and pour the chilled soymilk broth
   around the noodles.

7. Garnish with cucumbers, tomato, and a
   few sesame seeds for color.

Note: Kongguksu needs to be served cold.
You may want to add couple of ice cubes to
the dish when you serve the noodles.

Chef Catherine Shaffer

Chef Cathy Shaffer is the founder of Contemporary Korean Kitchen. Cathy was born in South Korea and came to America when she was nine years old. She has always loved Korean food, thanks to authentic Korean meals prepared by her mother. After a career in accounting, she embarked on a new path and pursued her passion for fine cuisine, graduating from the French Culinary Institute in New York City's Manhattan. Cathy worked at a number of restaurants in Manhattan and New Jersey, including Jean-Georges, Oriont, and Grand Cafe. She has spent the last twelve years traveling extensively as a sought-after private chef, working on board private yachts and visiting deserted islands, and preparing gourmet meals for business leaders, celebrities, and professional athletes, including CC Sabathia and other members of the New York Yankees.

About Soy Milk

"Milk" is really a misnomer since this liquid comes from a plant rather than a mammary gland of an animal, and that's why in Europe it's usually called "Soy Drink." Made from soy beans, soy milk has as much protein as cow's milk but little calcium unless it's enriched. Tofu can be made from the coagulated protein of soy milk just as cheese can be made from cow's milk. It's a good alternative for people who are lactose intolerant.

LOTUS LEAF KALGUKSU

Homemade lotus noodles with mushrooms, zucchini, and potato

Serves 2

7 dried shiitake mushrooms

2 oz/50 g dried kelp

3 tbsp soy sauce

1 sheet lotus leaf

4 cups/400 g flour

1 tsp salt

3 tbsp olive oil

¼ cup/30 g julienned carrots

2 fresh chestnuts, peeled and julienned

¼ cup/20 g julienned black rock mushrooms

½ potato, peeled and julienned

½ zucchini, julienned

Salt

1 tbsp sesame oil

Garnish: 1 lotus flower

Contemporary Korean Kitchen

Contemporary Korean Kitchen offers cooking classes in New York City dedicated exclusively to the fine art of Korean cuisine. In Korean life and culture, food is not just for satisfying hunger and sustaining life. It is a celebration of life.

Chef Venerable Dae Ahn

Venerable Dae Ahn is one of the world's most respected and well-known temple cuisine masters. She heads Geumdang Temple Food and Culture Institute and founded Balwoo Gongyang, a restaurant specializing in temple cuisine. A Buddhist nun with a PhD in dietetics, Venerable Dae Ahn is a sought-after temple food lecturer, frequent television guest, and author of two books.

1. Put shiitake mushroom and kelp into a pot with 5 cups/1.2 L of water and boil for 10 minutes. Take out the mushrooms and kelp and set aside.

2. Add soy sauce to the mushroom stock.

3. Cut lotus leaf into small strips and add to a blender with ½ cup/120 ml of water and blend well. Strain the lotus leaf and squeeze out extra liquid. Set aside.

4. In a bowl add flour, salt, olive oil, and the lotus leaf extract. Mix well to form a dough. Shape into a ball, then cover with plastic wrap and let it rest for 1 hour.

5. In a bowl, add julienne carrot with touch of salt and 1 drop of sesame oil and toss lightly, and sauté in a dry pan. Repeat with chestnuts, black mushrooms, potato, and zucchini.

6. Squeeze out excess water from the shiitake mushrooms (used for the stock). Julienne shiitake mushrooms, add salt and sesame oil, and sauté in dry pan.

7. Set all the prepared vegetables aside.

8. After dough rests, take it out of the plastic wrap. Generously dust a cutting board with flour and roll out the dough. Cut into thick strips with a knife.

9. Bring the stock to a boil and cook the noodles for few minutes until they are done.

10. To serve: In a big bowl, add the cooked noodles with broth. Top with lotus flower. Gently open each petal and carefully place each of the sautéed vegetables on the petals. Before eating the noodles, stir the flower gently to release the fragrant scent. Lotus flower is edible.

NABEYAKI UDON

A simple soup that can use almost any fresh vegetables

HINOKI
Japanese Restaurant • Sushi Bar

Hinoki

37 New Orleans Road
Hilton Head Island, SC 29928
(843) 785-9800

Cuisine: Japanese

Chef Teruyuki Suzuki

This authentic Japanese restaurant and sushi bar was opened on Hilton Head Island in 2001 by Hirofumi Ono and Teruyuki Suzuki.

Chef Teruyuki Suzuki

Suzuki was manager and head chef at Kurama Japanese Seafood and Steak House for more than 10 years before becoming co-owner, manager, and chef at Hinoki.

Serves 2

For the Broth:

36 oz/1.5 L water

2 pieces of thick dried seaweed (kombu) 3x3 in/7.5x7.5 cm squares

3 tsp soy sauce

¼ tsp salt

Slow boil all broth ingredients for 15 minutes.

8 oz/230 g frozen udon noodles

4 green onion stems, cut in half

3-4 shiitake mushrooms, sliced

¼ lb/113 g tofu, cut in large cubes

Other vegetables to taste: such as spinach, Napa cabbage

Sliced fish cakes, cut in half (optional)

1 egg

1. Cook frozen udon noodles for 2 minutes in the hot broth.

2. Then place the remaining ingredients, except egg, on top of noodles and cook for 5-6 minutes.

3. At the end of cooking, crack egg open and drop it on top of vegetables; poach, do not stir.

About Tofu

A vegetarian protein source made from soy beans, tofu does not have much flavor on its own but tends to absorb the flavors of whatever other ingredients it is cooked with. There are two kinds of tofu: firm and silken. Firm, found in the refrigerator section of the grocery store, is the one used most often in cooking and what you should use if a recipe doesn't specify a kind of tofu. Silken tofu is very soft and creamy and used for desserts, dressings and sauces. It comes in shelf-stable packaging that doesn't need to be refrigerated until after it is opened.

ONE-POT ASIAN NOODLES

Gluten-free, dairy-free, soy-free, peanut-free, corn-free

Serves 6

8 oz/230 g mai fun rice noodles

4 cups/950 ml chicken broth

1 cup/240 ml water

⅓ cup/80 ml mirin

¼ cup/60 ml coconut aminos*

3 dried shiitake mushrooms

1 7 in/17.5 cm stick dried kombu, optional

2 tbsp gluten-free fish sauce

1 tbsp minced ginger

¼ tsp salt

12-16 oz/230-450 g chicken breast, thinly sliced**

2-3 baby bok choy, chopped

1 small red bell pepper, stemmed and thinly sliced

4 oz/113 g sugar snap or snow peas

3 green onions, white part and some of the green, sliced on the diagonal

2 oz/60 g beech mushrooms, optional

½ cup/16 g chopped cilantro, optional for garnish

Sriracha sauce, optional for garnish

1. Prepare noodles al dente according to package directions. Rinse under cold water, drain, and set aside.

2. In a large pot combine broth, water, mirin, coconut aminos, shiitake mushrooms, kombu, fish sauce, ginger, and salt. Bring to a boil; cover and reduce to simmer. Cook 10-15 minutes or until mushrooms are tender.

3. Using a slotted spoon, remove kombu and discard. Remove shiitake mushrooms, slice thinly, and return to pot.

4. Arrange chicken, bok choy, bell pepper, peas, peas, green onions, and beech mushrooms in pot. Cover; cook 6-8 minutes or until chicken is cooked through.

5. Push chicken and veggies aside. Add prepared noodles to pot. Heat through and serve. Garnish with cilantro and sriracha sauce if desired.

*If soy is tolerated, gluten-free soy sauce may be used in place of coconut aminos.

**Other proteins may be substituted for chicken; suggestions include extra-firm tofu (for the soy tolerant); raw, peeled, and deveined shrimp; or thinly sliced steak.

Lexie's Kitchen

www.lexieskitchen.com

Chef Lexie Croft

lexieskitchen.com is a blog created by Lexie Croft and is dedicated to her son, whose health issues inspired Lexie to revisit the way she and her family eats. Her recipes are free of gluten, dairy, egg, excess sugar/fruit, and preservatives.

OROSHI KINOKO SOBA

Enjoy a taste of the sea with this bonito and seaweed broth soba noodle soup

Umi

3050 Peachtree Road NE, Suite 1
Atlanta, GA
(404) 841-0040

Cuisine: Japanese

Chef Fuyuhiko Ito

The name Umi is the phonetic equivalent of the Japanese word for *sea*.

About the Chefs

Fuyuhiko Ito's background in both traditional Japanese and classic French cuisine is reflected in the starters, soups, salads, sashimi, and specialty rolls. Ito's wife, pastry chef Lisa Matsuoka Ito, provides the desserts.

About Bonito

Bonito, frequently found in Japanese cookery, is a tuna-like fish that is dried. Shavings of bonito, along with kombu (seaweed) are the main ingredients of Dashi broth, which is the base of many soups, sauces, and noodle dishes. When placed on top of hot foods, the heat waves cause the thin shavings of bonito to move, giving the appearance of dancing on top of the dish.

Serves 4

For the Dashi Broth:

4 cups/950 ml water

8 in x 6 in/20 cm x 15 cm piece kombu seaweed

4 oz/113 g shaved bonito

½ cup/120 ml soy sauce

1. Put cold water and kombu into a pot.

2. Start heating on medium-low heat, so that the temperature doesn't increase dramatically. These 4 cups should take about 8 minutes to heat to 167°F/75°C.

3. When water reaches that temperature, you should start seeing small bubbles on the surface. When you see them, remove the kombu. Then skim off any white bubbles from the surface. This will give you a better-tasting broth.

4. After you remove the kombu, heat your broth to almost, but not quite, boiling. Turn off the heat and put all the shaved bonito in.

5. Leave at room temperature. The bonito will eventually sink to bottom of your pot. While the broth is cooling, try not to move it or it will become cloudy.

6. This process may take about an hour, or you can cool down the broth in 20 minutes by using an ice bath. Or prepare the broth the night before.

7. When broth is cold, add soy sauce.

1 package maitake mushrooms

1 package shimeji mushrooms

½ package shiitake mushrooms

1 package enoki mushrooms

1 package nametake mushrooms (optional)

½ cup/120 ml sake

1 lb/450 g daikon radish, peeled and grated

1 lb/450 g buckwheat soba noodles

1. Cut off bottoms of the stems of all the mushrooms and cut the mushrooms to preferred size.

2. Bring dashi broth and sake to a boil. Add mushrooms and radishes and boil for 2 minutes, then taste it. If it's too bland, add some salt. When done, strain and chill it in refrigerator.

3. Boil 1 gallon/2 liters of water. Add noodles and cook until done. Then submerge cooked noodles in ice water.

4. Place noodles in serving bowls. Reheat dashi and mushroom broths and pour over noodles. Serve.

PAD THAI TAO

Homemade Pad Thai sauce makes this dish extra delicious

TAO

42 E. 58th Street
New York, NY 10022
(212) 888-2288

Also a location in Las Vegas, Nevada

Cuisine: Japanese

Chef Ralph Scamardella

Originally a nineteenth-century stable for the Vanderbilt family, and then a balconied movie theater, TAO NY was transformed into a majestic Asian "temple."

Serves 2

7 oz/200 pad thai noodles, soaked in water
    and drained

¼ cup/60 ml peanut oil

2 eggs

1/2 cup/120 ml pad thai sauce

1 oz /30 g bean sprouts

1 oz /30 g firm tofu, sliced

1 oz /30 g green onions, chopped

1 oz/30 g shiitake mushrooms, sliced

¼ tsp preserved radish, shredded

¼ tsp dried shrimp, chopped

Garnish:

Chopped peanuts

¼ lime

Bean sprouts

Cilantro

Pad Thai Sauce

1 cup/240 ml tamarind sauce

8 oz/200 g palm sugar, crushed

½ cup/120 ml fish sauce

2 tsp salt

½ cup/120 ml water

½ cup/120 ml lime juice

Place all ingredients together in a saucepan and simmer for 45 minutes, stirring occasionally to make sure it does not scorch on the bottom.

1. Make pad thai sauce and set aside.
2. Cook pad thai noodles for 1 minute in boiling water.
3. Heat wok over high heat.
4. Add peanut oil; when the oil is hot, scramble eggs. Remove from pan and set aside.
5. Add sauce, carmelize slightly, add noodles and egg.
6. Cook for 10 seconds; add remaining ingredients.
7. Cook for 15 seconds more.

SAKURAMEN

Vegetarians and meat lovers alike will appreciate the smooth miso broth
and soy-marinated portabella mushrooms

Sakuramen

2441 18th Street NW
Washington, DC
202-656-5285

Cuisine: Korean, Japanese and Chinese

Chef M.E. Cho

The name "Sakuramen" is an combination of *sakura* (Japanese for cherry blossom) and *ramen*. Similarly, Sakuramen's menu is a hybrid of Korean, Japanese, and Chinese cuisine. A former communications tech at the Cancer Institute, Jonathan Cho, and his brother-in-law, Jay Park, a former production engineer in broadcast media who is studying oriental medicine, launched Sakuramen in 2012. What brought them together in this venture was their mutual love of ramen. When the restaurant opened, the entire family was in the kitchen—wives, mothers, and everyone else they could enlist.

Serves 4

For Menma Sauce:

½ cup/120 ml soy sauce

½ cup/120 ml water

3 tsp sugar

2 tsp mirin

Mix all ingredients together in a bowl.

For Marinade for Portabella Mushrooms:

1 tbsp soy sauce

1 tsp chopped green onions

1 tsp sesame oil

1 pinch ground sesame seeds

½ tbsp sugar

Mix all ingredients together in a bowl.

For Miso Tare:

Miso paste (best quality you can find)

Vegetable oil

Garlic, minced

Sugar

Mirin

Soy sauce

Sesame Oil

Sesame seeds

Black pepper

Ginger, minced

About Miso Tare: Every miso tare is different, according to the chef's desired taste, so feel free to experiment, but always start with the highest quality miso paste you can find (Japanese or Korean brands are usually best). Add small amounts of other ingredients until you reach your desired flavor.

In a small bowl, combine miso paste, vegetable oil, and remaining spices. Hand mix until you have an even, consistent paste.

For Hoseki Oil:

1 apple slice

1 clove garlic

1 ginger root

1 white onion

1. Finely chop all ingredients.

2. Pour ½ cup/120 ml vegetable oil in pan over medium-high heat until it starts to simmer.

3. Add all ingredients and reduce to medium heat. Simmer until browned.

4. Remove from heat and cool.

10 medium shiitake mushrooms
1 sheet kombu (3 x 5 in/7.5 x 12.5 cm size)
1 whole baby bamboo shoot
2 cups/200 g kernel corn

4 large portabella mushrooms (caps only), sliced ½ in/1.25 cm thick and finger length
1¼ lb/565 g freshest available thick curly ramen noodles (NOT dried)
4 tbsp miso paste
2 cups/120 g thinly sliced green onions

4 slices of nori (dried seaweed)
  (4 x 4 in/10 x 10 cm)

Chef M.E. Cho

The recipes for seven varieties of ramen, plus house-made dumplings and buns, come from Jonathan's wife, Myung Eun Cho. Despite the family's Korean roots, the food takes inspiration from a wide range of cultures.

1. Prepare menma sauce, marinade, miso tare, and hoseki oil.

2. In a large pot, pour in 1-1½ gal/5-6 L of water and add shiitake mushrooms and kombu. Soak for 8 to 12 hours.

3. Turn on high heat and bring to a boil.

4. As the kombu broth starts heating up, make the toppings.

5. For menma topping: Slice bamboo shoot approximately finger length/width and place in a pan. Pour menma sauce (that you made earlier) into pan with the bamboo shoots and simmer for 25 minutes over medium-low heat. Remove from heat and set aside in a small bowl to cool.

6. Roast corn kernels in greaseless pan over medium-high heat until slightly browned. Remove from pan and set aside to cool.

7. Preheat pan. Combine mushrooms and marinade in hot pan. Cook evenly on both sides until mushrooms are soft and tender and slightly browned.

8. In a separate large pot, boil water for noodles. Cook to desired consistency.

9. Pour approximately 2 ¼ cups/535 ml of piping hot kombu stock into a serving bowl.

10. Add 2 tbsp miso tare and miso paste to kombu stock and stir well. Add more tare for desired taste.

11. When noodles are done, drain well, and add to bowl with kombu/miso broth.

12. Add toppings: roasted corn, marinated mushrooms, and green onions.

13. Drizzle 1 tsp hoseki oil over top.

14. Insert 1 slice of nori into broth against the bowl. Serve while hot!

SCALLION CONFIT NOODLES

Sesame oil infuses the scallions with rich color and flavor

Mira Sushi & Izakaya

46 W. 22nd Street
New York, NY 10010
(212) 989-7889

Cuisine: Gourmet Asian Street Food

Chef Brian Tsao

This recently opened Flatiron-district
restaurant is overseen by Chef Brian,
along with sushi chef Owen Wu.

Serves 3

For the Sauce:

⅓ cup/80 ml soy sauce

2oz/60 g garlic, mashed to paste

⅛ cup/30 ml sesame oil

For the Scallion Confit:

1 cup/240 ml vegetable oil

1 bunch scallions, white section only,
    cut in half lengthwise

For the Noodles:

1 ½ lb/675 g fresh Chinese thin noodles

3 large eggs, fried sunny side up

½ bunch scallions, green section only,
    finely chopped (for garnish)

Chef Brian Tsao

Tsao, formerly of Telepan, comes from a Chinese-Korean background. His wife is Malaysian, and all of these different influences are reflected in the foods he prepares. Before graduating from the Culinary Institute of America, Tsao was a musician and traveled throughout Asia exploring different cuisines.

1. Combine soy sauce, garlic, and sesame oil, and let sit overnight to allow garlic to infuse the sauce.

2. Place the vegetable oil and green onion in a cooking pot and slowly bring up the temperature. When the oil begins to bubble, use a wooden spoon or set of long chopsticks to keep the scallions moving; this will prevent uneven browning. When the scallions are a light caramel color, remove from oil onto a bed of paper towels to stop the cooking and cool. (It is normal for the scallions to turn slightly darker in color even after removing from the oil.) Reserve the oil.

3. When scallions and oil cool off, combine them again and leave at room temperature for a scallion confit.

4. Cook noodles in a large pot of boiling water (water MUST be boiling). To check if the noodles are done, carefully pull out a piece and break it. If the center has a very small center of raw white dough, it will need another minute.

5. Once noodles are done, split between three bowls. Stir the soy sauce mixture well and pour 2 tbsp/60 ml into each bowl and top with scallion confit to taste. Mix some of the confit oil with the noodles to properly lubricate them.

6. Place a sunny side up egg on top of the noodles, garnish with chopped green scallions, and enjoy!

SESAME GINGER SALAD

Two kinds of cabbage make this dish pretty to look at, as well as delicious

House Foods

Chef Mai Pham

Mai Pham is the chef/owner of the nationally acclaimed Lemon Grass and Star Ginger restaurants in Sacramento, California. A recognized expert on Asian cuisine and industry leader, Chef Pham is known for her innovative, fresh take on Vietnamese, Thai and other Southeast Asian cooking. The author of several award-winning cookbooks as well as host of the TV Food Network *My Country, My Kitchen* series, she's a frequent guest chef instructor at The Culinary Institute of America. Chef Pham's recipes feature homestyle foods that she grew up with in Vietnam and Thailand, including dishes such as Mom's Catfish in Claypot. Chef Mai partnered with House Foods Tofu to create this savory and colorful Sesame Ginger Salad.

Serves 3–5

3 (8 oz/230 g) packages House Foods Tofu
    Shirataki, spaghetti shaped

½ cup/170 g green cabbage

½ cup/170 g red cabbage

½ cup/75 g carrot matchsticks

¼ cup/18 g mint leaves

¼ cup/8 g cilantro

½ cup/35 g spinach

1½ tsp sesame seeds

1.   Rinse and drain Tofu Shirataki noodles well. Pat dry using paper towels. Put in a microwave-safe bowl and heat in microwave for 1 minute. Drain excess liquid and pat dry. Cut noodles to manageable size.

2.   Combine noodles with dressing and toss several times. Set aside for at least 30 minutes for noodles to absorb flavors.

3.   To assemble salad, add cabbage, carrots, mint, and cilantro to noodle mixture and toss gently. Add spinach and toss gently again. Garnish with sesame seeds and serve.

Ginger Dressing

1½ tbsp chopped fresh ginger

2 tbsp vinegar

2½ tbsp sugar

2 tbsp soy sauce

2 tsp sesame oil

Place all dressing ingredients in a blender except for the oil and process just until smooth. Add the oil and continue processing until well blended. Set aside.

SPICY BASIL NOODLES

The combination of several vegetables make this a hearty dish

koh
by Ian Kittichai

Koh

Intercontinental City Hotel
135 Marine Drive
Mumbai 40020 India
91 22 3987 9999

Cuisine: Thai

Chef Ian Kittichai

"High Thai" cuisine can be enjoyed in a plush and exotic setting in the Intercontinental Marine Drive Hotel in Mumbai. This is Chef Kittichai's fourth restaurant, having opened in 2010.

Serves 2

7 oz/200 g flat rice noodles

1 oz/20 g broccoli florets

1 oz/20 g snow peas

½ oz /15 g haricot string beans

¼ oz/5 grams Thai basil leaves

2 tbsp onion, finely chopped

1¾ tbsp garlic, minced

1 tsp green peppercorns

4 stems bok choy

1 oz/20 g straw mushroom

4 tsp vegetable stock

4 tsp oyster sauce

Sugar, to taste

½ tbsp soy sauce

1. Soak rice noodles in warm water for 10-15 minutes.

2. Blanch broccoli florets, snow peas, and haricot beans in hot boiling water .

3. Deep-fry hot basil leaves and drain on a kitchen towel.

4. Heat a little oil in a wok. Add onion and garlic and sauté till the onions are translucent.

5. Add green peppercorns and sauté for 30 seconds.

6. Add all the vegetables and vegetable stock and cook for a several minutes until vegetables are done.

7. Finally add soaked noodles, oyster sauce, and sugar. Mix thoroughly.

8. Serve hot, drizzled with soy sauce and garnished with fried basil leaves.

Chef Ian Kittichai

Chef Ian Kittichai's path to culinary success started from very humble beginnings in Bangkok. Every morning he would rise at 3 a.m. to accompany his mother to the wet market to select the best meats, seafood, and vegetables for her neighborhood grocery. While Ian was at school, she would cook a dozen different types of curries. Upon his return home, Ian would push a cart through the neighborhood to sell his wares, shouting: "Khow Geang Ron Ron Ma Leaw Jaar!" (Hot curry coming!)

About Thai Basil

Thai basil has some distinct differences from its more common cousin, sweet basil: It has purplestems and spear-shaped leaves instead of the wide leaves and green stem found with Sweet Basil. Most important for cooking, the flavor of Thai basil is able to stand up to high heat and extended cooking times.

STIR-FRIED GREEN BEAN VERMICELLI

Lots of fresh green vegetables make this a perfect springtime offering

MEИTAPHOR

Mehtaphor

130 Duane Street
New York, NY 10013
(212) 542-9440

Cuisine: Eclectic

Chef Jehangir Mehta

If metaphor is a figure of speech that compares two unlike things that actually have something in common, *Mehtaphor* is inspired by Asian urban tastes and scents and wrapped in Jehangir Mehta's singular chef voice.

Serves 4

8-10 asparagus stalks, cut in pieces on the bias

8 oz/230g green bean vermicelli (glass noodles)

1½ tbsp olive oil

1 tsp cumin seeds

1 tbsp mustard seeds

1 Thai green chili, split in two pieces

1 Thai red long chili, sliced

1 fresh turmeric, chopped

4 cloves garlic, chopped

4 scallions, chopped, green and white part separated

2 king mushrooms, diced

1 cup/150g edamame beans

1½ cups/50g baby spinach

½ bunch chives, finely chopped

½ bunch cilantro, finely chopped

1 tsp ground black pepper

1 lime, cut in quarters

1. Bring water to a boil.

2. Add asparagus to the water and boil for 3 minutes. Then remove to a bowl with a slotted spoon.

3. To the same boiling water add salt to taste and the vermicelli. Remove from heat and let rest in the pot for 4 minutes. Drain the vermicelli and add ½ tbsp of the olive oil so that it doesn't stick. Set aside.

4. In a fry pan, heat the rest of olive oil on medium-high heat. Add the cumin seeds. mustards seeds, 2 chilies, turmeric, and garlic.

5. Stir-fry 1 minute, then add the white part of the scallions and the mushrooms.

6. Stir-fry 2 minutes more, then add the asparagus and edamame.

7. Add the vermicelli and stir for 30 seconds. Then add the spinach, chives, and cilantro.

8. Divide into four bowls. Season with salt and pepper. Squeeze 1 lime quarter over each serving and sprinkle on green parts of scallion.

STIR-FRIED NOODLES WITH PEANUT SAUCE

A super speedy version of this popular dish

Serves 6

1 lb/450 g rice noodles (sometimes called rice sticks or Bahn Pho) or gluten-free fettuccini

2 tbsp vegetable oil

7 oz/225 g shiitake mushrooms, cleaned, stemmed, and sliced into ¼ inch/.5 cm pieces

2 red bell peppers, stemmed, seeded and deveined, thinly sliced

6 green onions, trimmed and cut into 1 inch/2.5 cm pieces; white and green parts separated

¾ cup/180 ml San-J Thai Peanut Sauce

1. Cook the noodles in salted boiling water according to the package directions, stirring often with a fork to keep the noodles separated. Drain and rinse well under hot water.

2. Heat the oil over high heat in a large skillet or wok until it shimmers.

3. Add the mushrooms, peppers, and white part of the green onions and cook for 2 minutes, stirring often.

4. Add the drained noodles, green part of the green onions, and San-J Thai Peanut Sauce. Continue to cook, stirring constantly, for another 2 minutes or until the noodles have absorbed most of the sauce. Serve immediately.

Chef Carol Kicinski

Carol Kicinski is a professional recipe developer, television chef, magazine founder and editor-in-chief, freelance writer, and cookbook author—who cooks, writes, and travels, doing it all gluten-free! She prides herself in creating recipes that are not just "good for gluten-free," but just plain good! Her blog, simplygluten-free.com, is designed to share, teach, and inspire with gluten-free recipes.

THAI INSPIRED NOODLES WITH PEANUT SAUCE

A healthy makeover for sesame noodles

the *picky*eater

The Picky Eater

www.pickyeaterblog.com

Chef Anjali Shah

Chef Anjali Shah

The Picky Eater (pickyeaterblog.com) is a healthy food blog created by Anjali Shah. She describes herself as a "whole wheat" health-conscious girl who married a "white bread" fast-food guy. Anjali made it her mission to "sneak" healthy foods into her husband's diet that were so delicious that her husband wouldn't even realize he was changing he way he eats!

Serves 6

Olive oil cooking spray

Half a block of firm tofu (from a 16oz/450 g pack), cut in bite-sized pieces

1 red pepper, diced

⅓ cup/20 g green onions, sliced

3 cloves garlic, chopped

8 oz/230 g whole wheat spaghetti

1 package frozen broccoli florets (10 oz /150 g package)

2 tbsp soy sauce

⅓ cup of crunchy peanut butter (you can substitute purchased satay peanut sauce if you're not a strict vegetarian and if you don't want to make the peanut sauce from scratch!)

3 tbsp light coconut milk

Thai red curry paste to taste

1 tbsp sesame seeds, plus more to garnish

A pinch of crushed red pepper, to taste

1. Coat a large pan with cooking spray. Heat over medium heat, then toss the tofu in. Lightly fry the tofu until it's slightly browned.

2. Then add the red pepper, green onions and garlic.

3. Cook spaghetti according to package directions.

4. While the spaghetti is cooking, add the frozen broccoli, soy sauce, peanut butter, coconut milk, and thai red curry paste (or eliminate the coconut milk and thai red curry paste if using the satay peanut sauce) to the tofu mixture.

5. Once the spaghetti is done, transfer the noodles to the veggie mixture and stir to combine.

6. Sprinkle on the sesame seeds and stir them in well.

7. Add the crushed red pepper to taste and heat through. Add soy sauce or salt to taste.

Quick Tip

Make sure your peanut butter is at room temperature, so it easily combines with the rest of the ingredients! Otherwise you'll be waiting for a while for it to heat through.

TRADITIONAL PHUD THAI

Made with rice noodles, tamarind, and fish sauce

Salad King

340 Yonge Street
Toronto, ON M5B 1R8
Canada
(416) 593-03333

Cuisine: Thai

A favorite venue for Ryerson students, Salad King has been serving Thai food in Toronto for over 20 years.

Serves 2

For Phud Thai Sauce:
2 oz/40 g tamarind
1 cup/200 ml water
¼ cup/50 g plum sugar
1 tbsp/15 ml fish sauce
Salt and sugar to taste

1. Soak the tamarind in the water for 30 minutes. Knead tamarind in water until it breaks up and has thoroughly combined with the water. Strain mixture into a small bowl. Discard tamarind solids.

2. Put the tamarind water, plum sugar, and fish sauce in a small saucepan and stir over low heat until the plum sugar has dissolved. Add salt and sugar to taste. Set aside.

For Phud Thai Stir-Fried Noodles:
8 oz/230 g rice noodles (wet weight)
1 tsp vegetable oil
1 egg
Phud Thai sauce (above)
4 oz/113 g bean sprouts
2 green onions, sliced
2 oz/60 g tofu, cut into small cubes
1 tbsp unsalted peanuts
Lime
Coriander

1. You can either use fresh rice noodles or dry rice noodles for phud thai. To use dry rice noodles, soak the noodles in cold water for 2 hours, or warm water for 1 hour.

2. Heat a wok over high heat until a drop of water sizzles and dances when dropped in the wok. Add vegetable oil and evenly coat the wok bottom.

3. Add the egg to the hot wok, and scramble.

4. Add the noodles to the wok and stir-fry until the noodles have softened (approximately 1 minute).

5. Add the phud thai sauce, bean sprouts, green onion, and tofu to the noodles. Stir-fry until the sauce has thickened and has a light golden color.

6. Remove the phud thai from the heat. Plate the noodles, topping them with peanuts, lime, and coriander to garnish. Optional: Add strips of chicken breast.

VEGAN SAIGON SOUP

Sambal brings the "hot" and tamarind brings the "sour" to this hot and sour soup

Saigon Kitchen

526 West State Street
Ithaca, NY 14850
(607) 257-8881

Cuisine: Vietnamese

Chefs Bill Lam and Phouc Tran

The Lam family opened the doors to Saigon Kitchen in 2011 to introduce authentic Vietnamese food to Ithaca, New York. With the belief that great food and cooking brings family, friends and loved ones together, the Lam family took a chance and opened what is now one of the hottest places to grab a bite in Ithaca—a restaurant that is home to foodies and adventurous diners.

Serves 2

½ tsp minced fresh garlic

1 tsp vegetable oil

3 ½ cups/820 ml vegetable stock

½ tbsp sambal

½ stalk lemongrass, crushed and chopped thin

1 tbsp tamarind base mix

½ cup/100 g sugar

1 8-oz/230 g package of soft tofu

½ cup/80 g celery, sliced thin and diagonally

¼ cup/45 g fresh pineapple, sliced

1 8oz/230 g package of vermicelli noodles

½ cup/50 g bean sprouts

1 ripened vine tomato, diced

Garnish:

1 scallion, thinly sliced

1 tbsp cilantro

1 jalapeño, seeded and sliced thin (optional)

1. In a medium-sized pot, heat garlic in oil over low heat until fragrant.

2. Add vegetable stock, sambal, lemongrass, tamarind base, and sugar and bring to a boil. Lower heat and simmer and for 10-15 minutes, stirring occasionally.

3. Add tofu, celery, and pineapple. Simmer for 3-5 minutes.

4. Add vermicelli noodles and cook for approximately one minute.

5. Divide bean sprouts and tomatoes into two soup bowls. Ladle the soup into the bowls and garnish with scallions, cilantro, and jalapeño. Serve immediately.

About Sambal

This seasoning/condiment has a chili base and is extremely hot. Sometimes it is used in place of fresh chili peppers. Sambal can be found ready-made. Other flavors in the sauce can be shrimp paste, fish sauce, garlic, ginger, shallots, green onions, sugar, lime juice, and rice or other vinegars.

VEGETABLE PEANUT NOODLES

Zesty-flavored noodles with lots of crunchy vegetables

Pondicher

2800 Kirby Drive B132
Houston, TX 77098
(713) 522-2022

Cuisine: Indian

Chef Anita Jaisinghani

Pondicheri is the name of a small coastal town, off the Bay of Bengal in South India (known also as Pondicherry or Podcherry), where Anita was a frequent visitor in her childhood days and it has special memories for her.

Serves 2

4 cups/225 g Chinese thin rice noodles

3 tbsp sesame oil

3-4 clove garlic, chopped

2 small carrots, julienned

1 red bell pepper, thinly sliced

1 stalk celery, thinly sliced on the bias

1 small red onion, thinly sliced

2 in/5 cm piece ginger, julienned

2 tsp black pepper

2 tsp salt

4 tbsp Shaoxing cooking wine or
  rice wine vinegar

Zest and juice from 1 orange

2 tbsp ketchup manis (Indonesian soy sauce)

1 tsp Szechuan peppercorns, ground

2 tbsp sambhal olek (Indonesian chili sauce)

2 tbsp peanut butter

2 cups/135 g spinach leaves, sliced

1 cup/340 g purple cabbage, sliced

2 tbsp chopped cilantro

2 tbsp toasted and chopped peanuts

1. Pour boiling water over the noodles and let them soak for 3-4 minutes. Drain and set aside.

2. In a large wok or sauté pan, heat up the sesame oil and add the garlic. Almost immediately, add the julienned carrots and cook for 4-5 minutes, frequently stirring.

3. Add the red bell peppers and cook for another minute. Turn up heat and cook, stirring on high for 2-3 minutes.

4. Add the celery, red onions, ginger, black pepper, and salt. Cook for just under another minute and add the cooking wine, orange juice with zest, ketchup manis, peppercorns, sambhal olek, and peanut butter. Continue cooking at high heat for 2-3 minutes or until the sauce around the vegetables is bubbly.

5. Add the noodles, spinach, cabbage, cilantro, and peanuts. Toss to mix, turn the heat off, and serve immediately.

Chef Anita Jaisinghani

Anita Jaisinghani was born and raised in India. An avid traveler and reader, her true passion is creativity in food. She harnesses her scientific background to experiment with ideas that blend flavors of her native Sindh culture with local Texas ingredients, using techniques she has learned through her childhood and her travels.

About Rice Wine

Aged for 10 years or more, rice wine is a rich-flavored liquid that is made by fermenting rice or millet. Since the best and most famous rice wines have come from Shaoxing, it is sometimes called Shaoxing Cooking Wine. For rice vinegar, the fermentation process is taken one step further and the alcohol in the wine is turned into an acid.

VEGETARIAN PAD THAI NOODLES

Rice noodles with eggs and bok choy

OUTRIGGER
LAGUNA PHUKET
RESORT AND VILLAS

Panache

142/3 Moo 6, Laguna Village
Cherngtalay, Phuket 83110,
Thailand
66 76 336 900

Cuisine: Thai

Chef Robert Czeschka

At Panache Restaurant, guests experience poolside, al fresco, and indoor dining with a spectacular interactive kitchen concept. The International and Asian cuisine emphasizes casual, creative, and healthy preparations, and offers a delightful spin on made-to-order meals where chefs prepare dishes to a customer's particular preference.

Serves 2

8 oz/230g dried pad thai rice noodles, (linguini-width)

1-2 eggs (vegans can substitute ½ cup soft tofu)

3-4 tbsp oil for stir-frying

4 green onions, white parts sliced and kept separate from green

3 cloves garlic, minced

1 tsp. grated galangal or ginger

1 fresh red or green chili, sliced

3-4 baby bok choy, or equivalent amount of other Chinese cabbage, roughly chopped

¼ cup/60 ml vegetable stock

2-3 cups/200-300 g bean sprouts

⅓ cup/11 g fresh coriander/cilantro

¼ cup/40 g chopped unsalted dry-roasted peanuts; or substitute cashews

Lime wedges for serving

For Pad Thai Sauce

¾ to 1½ tbsp tamarind paste

3½ tbsp soy sauce or wheat-free soy sauce

½ to 1 tsp chili sauce (to taste)

3 tbsp brown sugar (or more to taste)

⅛ tsp ground white pepper

Chef Robert Czeschka

Chef Czescha is an Austrian national with twenty-six years of experience, including sixteen years as an Executive Chef in Germany, Egypt, Malaysia, Thailand, China, and most recently at the luxury Nam Hai Resort in Hoi An, Vietnam.

1. Bring a pot of water to a boil and turn off heat. Soak noodles in the hot water for 4-6 minutes, or until limp but still too firm to eat. Drain and rinse with cold water. Note: Noodles must be under-cooked at this stage.

2. Combine Pad Thai Sauce ingredients and tofu, if using instead of eggs, in a cup, stirring well to dissolve the paste and sugar (if tamarind paste is thick, only add 1 tbsp; if thin and runny, add 1 ½ tbsp). Set aside.

3. Warm a wok or large frying pan over medium-high heat. Add 1–2 tbsp oil plus the white parts of the green onion, garlic, galangal/ginger, and chili. Stir-fry 1 minute to release the fragrance.

4. Add the bok choy and vegetable stock. Stir-fry 2 minutes, or until bok choy is bright green and slightly softened.

5. Push ingredients aside and add ½ tbsp more oil to the center of the wok/pan. Add the egg and stir-fry briefly to scramble.

6. Once the pan is dry, push ingredients aside and add a little more oil to the middle. Add the drained noodles and ⅓ of the sauce. Stir-fry everything together for 1-2 minutes with a gently tossing motion. Keep heat between medium-high and high, reducing if noodles begin to stick or burn. Keep adding sauce and continue stir-frying in this way 2-3 more minutes, or until sauce is gone and noodles are soft but still chewy (al dente) and a little sticky.

7. Remove from heat and add the bean sprouts, folding them into the hot noodles. Taste-test, and adjust seasoning: add more soy sauce for a saltier flavor. If too salty or sweet for your taste, add a good squeeze of lime juice. If too sour, sprinkle over a little more sugar.

8. To serve, scoop noodles onto a serving platter. Sprinkle with reserved green onion, cilantro, and chopped nuts. Serve with wedges of fresh-cut lime. Thai chili sauce can also be served on the side for those who like their noodles extra spicy. Serve immediately and enjoy!

Note that this sauce should have a very strong-tasting flavor with sour-sweet first, followed by salty and spicy.

COMBINATIONS

COLD GREEN TEA SOBA NOODLES WITH SESAME SAUCE

A refreshing summer dish featuring chicken and crab

Bamboo Izakaya

1541 Ocean Ave, Ste 120
Santa Monica, CA 90401
(310) 566-3860

Cuisine: Japanese

Chef Toshio Sakamaki

Located on Ocean Avenue in Santa
Monica, Bamboo Izakaya offers classic
Japanese pub fare, a full sushi bar, and
off-the-grill specialties, all with an
unforgettable view!

Chef Toshio Sakamaki

Born into a family of Japanese restaurateurs in Tokyo, Japan, Toshio Sakamaki's skill for preparing Japanese cuisine has been a life-long pursuit steeped in tradition. After graduating high school in 1984, Sakamaki moved to New York, where he joined the culinary team as Sushi Chef at Hatsuhana, the first Japanese restaurant awarded four stars by *The New York Times*.

After four years in New York, Sakamaki moved to the West Coast and joined Goro's Robata Grill in Mill Valley, California, where he worked as Sushi Chef and Assistant Head Chef. Sakamaki brought his expertise to San Francisco in 1992, where he was trained in the Kaiseki-style of Japanese multi-course dining at Ichirin restaurant. Five years later, Sakamaki returned to Mill Valley's Robata Grill, this time as Partner and Executive Chef.

Sakamaki joined the Ozumo team in San Francisco in 2006, where he honed his skills in the preparation of sushi and sashimi and formal Kaiseki-style dining, as well as Asian fusion cuisine.

In 2013, Sakamaki moved to Santa Monica, California, to join Bamboo Izakaya as Executive Chef where he is continuing to prepare traditional cuisine, as well as creative interpretations of Japanese favorites.

Serves 5

For the Noodles:
20 oz/560 g green tea soba noodles
½ chicken breast
3 eggs
10 cooked crab legs or crab cakes
½ hot house cucumber, julienned
Kaiware (radish sprouts), optional

For the Sauce:
5 tsp sesame paste
5 tsp soy sauce
1 tsp sesame oil
6 tsp sugar
¼ tsp grated ginger
¼ tsp chili paste
1 tsp rice vinegar
10 tsp olive oil
10 tsp water

1. Cook soba noodles in boiling water, approximately 5 minutes. Then rinse with cold water and drain.

2. Mix all sauce ingredients, except olive oil and water. Slowly add olive oil and keep mixing, until sauce thickens, then add water. Chill.

3. Boil chicken breast meat and then shred.

4. Beat the eggs and use nonstick pan to make thin egg crepes. You should have enough to make 3 or 4 sheets. Julienne the crepes.

5. Remove meat from cooked crab legs or crab cakes and shred.

6. Keep all ingredients refrigerated and cold until ready to serve.

7. When ready to eat, mix all ingredients, top with radish sprouts, if using, and enjoy! Alternatively, you can place each item on the plate separately and serve sauce on the side, letting diners combine things as they wish.

DAN-Z NOODLE

This pork and shrimp dish was originally concocted by a poor fisherman
and sold as street food in Taiwan one hundred years ago

Serves 10

For Pork Bone Soup:

2¼ lb/1 kg pork bones

20 cups/1 dcl water

50 shrimp

5 tbsp oil

1 cup/80 g shallot, minced

3 green onions, chopped

2lb/900 g ground pork

2 tsp sugar

1 cup/240 ml soy sauce

2 tbsp rice wine

1 chicken bouillon cube (optional)

8 portions Taiwanese oil noodles

Chinese parsley, for garnish

Chef Theresa Lin

Lin, who has been called the "Julia Child of
Taiwan," is the author of sixteen cookbooks
in Chinese, was food designer of Ang Lee's
movie *Eat Drink Man Woman,* and is host of
What's Cooking, a daily radio show based in Los
Angeles. Lin was catering director of the movie
Life of Pi.

1. Prepare pork bone soup stock: Boil pork bones in water and cook down until the soup is reduced by about a quarter.

2. Add shrimp and cook for 2 minutes. Remove shrimp and peel. Put aside.

3. Cook shrimp shells in the soup for 30 minutes. Remove shells.

4. Make the pork sauce: Heat oil in a wok. Stir-fry the minced shallot and green onion in the oil for about 3 minutes or until fragrant.

5. Add the pork and stir-fry until it turns white.

6. Add sugar and soy sauce and continue stir-frying until you create an aroma.

7. Add wine and bring to a boil. Add 2 cups/475 ml pork bone soup stock. Cook for about 2 hours over low heat. (For richer flavor, add 1 chicken bouillon cube.)

8. Cook Taiwanese oil noodles in boiling water around 1 minute till done. Drain noodles and place in bowls. Add 1 cup/240 ml of pork-shrimp soup. Pour 3 tbsp pork sauce on top. Decorate with 1 shrimp and some Chinese parsley.

9. Serve brown vinegar, white pepper, and smashed garlic paste on the side and let each person add to suit individual taste.

DRUNKEN NOODLES

This versatile recipe can be made with beef, pork, or chicken

Serves 2

For the Sauce:

1 tbsp mushroom soy sauce

2 tbsp sweet soy sauce

1 tbsp oyster sauce

1½ tbsp fish sauce

1 tbsp sugar

1 tsp siracha sauce

1 tsp minced garlic

6-8 Thai basil leaves, chiffonade

3 tbsp canola or peanut oil

2-3 clove garlic, minced

2 eggs

⅓ lb/150 g beef, pork, or chicken, thinly sliced against the grain

½ medium white onion, sliced

1-2 serrano chiles, sliced thin

½ lb/230 g fresh rice noodles, separated

¼ cup/60 ml Chinese rice wine

1 cup/65 g Thai basil leaves, loosely packed

3-4 grape tomatoes, halved

1. Combine sauce ingredients in a small bowl and set aside.

2. Heat oil to medium high in a medium sauté pan and sauté garlic until light brown.

3. Add eggs and lightly scramble until barely set.

4. Add meat, onions, and chilies, folding constantly until the meat is half cooked, about 1 to 2 minutes.

5. Add fresh rice noodles and sauce. Toss to combine for about 3 to 5 minutes. Make sure the noodles are cooked until the edges are slightly crisp.

6. Deglaze pan with rice wine, and then add basil and tomatoes. Serve hot.

Chef Jet Tila

Tila is a chef and consultant as well as a teacher and student in the art of food. His numerous accomplishments in the culinary world continue to grow. This year alone, Tila has partnered with the Compass Group to launch Modern Asian Kitchen, a new fast-casual Pan-Asian concept with locations nationwide. He is also set to separately open Kuma Snowcream, a shaved-ice concept launching in Las Vegas this spring, all while continuing to build on his extensive national TV and radio appearances as a guest judge on *Chopped*, as well as hosting his own radio show on KLAA in Los Angeles.

DUCK CONFIT WITH RICE NOODLE SALAD AND PHO BROTH

A broth richly flavored with chicken, pork, and many herbs and spices
is the base for this duck-and-noodle soup

ROUGE ET BLANC
48 MACDOUGAL ST · NYC

Rouge et Blanc

48 Macdougal Street
New York, NY 10012
(212) 260-5757

Cuisine: French, American,
Vietnamese

Chefs Bryan Kidwell and
Macks Collins

The name Rouge and Blanc is
at once an homage to the wines
of France and to the classic
Stendhal novel. The restaurant
has the look and feel of a
French colonial tavern from
1940s Saigon.

For Pho Broth:

3 white onions, rough chopped

3 whole cloves garlic, crushed

10 bunches green onions, rough
chopped

1 whole chicken

5 lbs/2.2 kg chicken feet

5 lbs/2.2 kg pork bones

5 lbs/2.2 kg pork breast

5 kafir lime leaves

1 lb/450 g ginger, rough chopped

⅓ cup/30 g cloves

15 pieces star anise

12 sticks cinnamon

1 bunch cilantro

1 bunch Thai basil

1 bunch mint

2 stalks lemongrass, rough
chopped

8 thai bird chilies, rough chopped

Fish sauce

Lime juice

For Noodle Salad:

Napa cabbage

White onion

Green onions

Thai bird chili

Mint

Cilantro

Thai basil

Bean sprouts

2 lb/900 g noodles

Duck Confit:

Cure : 1 cup/200 g sugar,
2 cups/480 g salt, 1 bunch
cilantro chopped

Duck thighs, one per serving

Duck fat

For Thai Oil:

½ pint cilantro

½ pint Thai basil

½ pint mint

2 bunches green onions

1 clove garlic

1 thai bird chili

1 tsp salt

1 cup/240 ml grape seed oil

Process all the herbs, green
onions, garlic, chili, and salt in
a blender. Slowly add the oil
into the blender and continue
blending. Blend the oil for about
5 minutes straight, allowing the
liquids from the herbs to come
out and for the color to darken.

Serves 8

To Make the Pho Broth:

1. In a large stockpot, sweat vegetables until tender.

2. Add the whole chicken, chicken feet, pork bones, and pork breast into stockpot and pour water over it to cover.

3. Add herbs and spices. Bring the water to a boil, then turn the heat back down and let the liquid simmer. Skim the fat every so often. Add hot water as needed to keep bones and vegetables submerged. Simmer uncovered for 12-14 hours.

4. Strain stock through a fine mesh strainer into another large stockpot or heatproof container, discarding the solids. Cool immediately in large cooler of ice, or a sink full of ice water, to below 40°F/4.5°C Place in refrigerator overnight.

5. Remove solidified fat from surface of liquid.

6. Reheat and season the broth with fish sauce and lime juice to taste.

To Make the Noodle Salad:

1. Thinly slice the napa cabbage, white and green onions, and thai bird chilies. Then finely chop mint, cilantro, and Thai basil. Add bean sprouts and mix.

2. Divide noodles among servings bowls. For each bowl, take a liberal handful of salad mix and add on top of noodles.

3. Pour hot broth on top to cook the vegetables.

To Make the the Duck Confit:

1. Mix the cure base together in a bowl, making sure all the ingredients are distributed evenly.

2. Coat the duck thighs in the cure mix and wrap it in plastic wrap for 8 hours.

3. Wash the cure off the duck thighs.

4. Melt duck fat in a saucepan over medium heat. Once the duck fat reaches about 200°F/95°C, pour over cured duck thighs. Wrap in aluminun foil and place in a 200°F/95°C oven. The ducks should be finished confitting after around 6 hours. Check the duck for tenderness: the thigh bone should pull out easily, which is a sign that the confitting is finished.

5. Place thighs in a skillet over medium heat and slowly render the duck skin until crispy.

6. Once crispy, place the duck skin side down on a towel and press out the excess fat.

7. Place the duck on top of the noodles and vegetables in the broth.

8. Add a few drops of the thai oil, to taste.

Chefs Bryan Kidwell and Macks Collins

Collins and Kidwell offer an East-meets-West French- and Vietnamese-inspired menu.

LAKSA LEMAK

This light yet creamy version of Laksa is enriched by the use of coconut milk
and a punchy rich spice paste

Banana Tree

103 Wardour Street
W1F 0UQ London
England
44 20 7437 1351

Multiple locations in London

Cuisine: Indochinese

Chef William Chow

Serves 4

For Spice Paste:

½ oz/15 g of garlic

1 cup/150 g of onions

4 stalks of lemongrass, discard the dried leafy
tops and finely chopped

⅓ cup/40 g of galangal
(substitute ginger as alternative)

2 tsp chili powder (omit if you don't like the
heat but increase the paprika below)

2 tsp paprika

1 tsp shrimp paste

1 tbsp dried shrimps (soaked and drained)

1 tbsp madras curry powder

½ tsp salt

⅓ cup/75ml vegetable oil for frying Spice Paste

Banana Tree showcases the best dishes from
various Southern Asian countries, including
Vietnam, Laos, Cambodia, Thailand, Malaysia,
and Singapore.

Chef William Chow

Chow opened his first Banana Tree cafe in
1991 and now has six restaurants in London
with a special interest in providing great healthy
food from a variety of Asian cuisines. His
restaurants now also serve as an "in-house"
chef training academy.

1. Mix all ingredients together until it
   becomes a paste. I recommend using a
   wet spice grinder for this job; otherwise,
   use a traditional stone pounder. Add
   a little oil, if necessary, to help the paste
   grind more easily.

2. Heat oil in a deep frying pan and slowly
   fry the spice paste, constantly stirring the
   bottom of the pan to stop the paste from
   sticking to the bottom.

3. Add more oil, if necessary, to help the
   frying process. The paste is ready when the
   oil starts to separate from the solids.

For the Stock:

1½ qt/1½ L chicken stock

6-8 tbsp of Asian fish sauce (adjust to taste)

1 can coconut milk (available from most
Asian food shops)

1 tbsp sugar

For the Soup:

1¾ lb/800 g fresh yellow wheat noodles,
blanched and drained (you can literally use
any type of noodles or even Italian pasta—
they will all work well)

Accompaniments:

3½ cups/360 g beansprouts, blanched
for 20 seconds and drained

12 pieces fried bean curd (available from most
Asian food shops)

1 large aubergine, cut in 2 in/5 cm cubes,
deep-fried and drained

1 lb/400 g chicken (roasted or boiled),
cold and hand shredded

12 tiger prawns, medium size, peeled and
blanched

Be flexible with the ingredients. There is no
shame in omitting or replacing ingredients
from this section with meat and/or vegetables
of your preference. For example, if broccoli is
your thing, go ahead and put in some broccoli,
but do blanch it first.

Garnish:

2 tbsp crispy fried shallots (available from most
Asian shops)

2 tbsp chopped coriander

1 tbsp chopped spring onions

1. To make the soup, add the spice paste
and the stock together and gently heat
the mixture. Make sure it does not get to
a violent rolling boil, as the oil from the
coconut cream will separate. It is normal to
have a small layer of aromatic spice oil on
the surface of the soup. Note: Always taste
your stock and adjust the salt and sugar
levels to your taste.

2. To assemble: Put the noodles and the
accompaniments into your individual
serving bowls and gently pour in the
piping hot stock.

3. Finish by sprinkling on the garnishes.
Enjoy.

MAMA MIEN

Shrimp and chicken star in this dish with a seafood-flavored sauce

Serves 2

1 tbsp oyster sauce

1 tbsp fish sauce

1 tbsp soy sauce

1 tsp sugar

3 tbsp water

1 tsp sesame oil

8 oz/230 g boiled egg noodles

1oz/28 g julienned cucumber

1oz/28 g julienned carrot

1oz/28 g gently boiled bean sprouts

1 tbsp chopped onion

3oz/85 g ground chicken

3oz/85 g peeled and deveined shrimp

1 tsp crab paste

1 tsp garlic chili paste

1. Combine oyster sauce, fish sauce, soy sauce, sugar, and water. Set aside.

2. Preheat sauté pan over high heat. Add ½ tsp sesame oil. Stir-fry cooked noodles for about 2 minutes. Transfer to serving plate.

3. Top noodles with cucumber, carrots, and beansprouts. Set aside.

4. In the same pan, add the rest of the sesame oil and the chopped onion. Sauté until fragrant.

5. Add ground chicken and cook for about 2 minutes, or until 80% cooked.

6. Add shrimp and continue to stir-fry for about a minute.

7. Add crab paste, garlic chili paste, and sauce. Bring sauce almost to a boil, and pour over cooked noodles. Serve.

9021Pho

490 N. Beverly Drive
Beverly Hills, California 90210
(310) 275-5277

Cuisine: Modern Vietnamese

Chef Kimmy Tang

This unique restaurant caters to the health conscious food-lover, featuring Asian recipes with French influences and California-inspired flair.

Chef Kimmy Tang

A pioneer in Asian fusion cuisine with over three decades of culinary experience, Kimmy was born and raised in Vietnam before fleeing to California after the fall of Saigon. She perfected her culinary skills in Chinese and Japanese restaurants in California, while learning English and completing her education, after which she traveled extensively, studying the cuisine of Greece, Hungary, Spain, Romania, France, Italy, and Germany. In Romania, Chef Kimmy became a culinary consultant for Romania's largest film studio. She also hosted a popular local TV cooking show. Inspired by her time abroad, Chef Kimmy came back to the United States in 2009 and opened her first pho restaurant, 9021Pho, in Beverly Hills.

MEE BANDUNG

The term "bandung" is not derived from Bandung, Indonesia, but is a term for anything that is mixed from many ingredients—as this recipe clearly shows, with its combination of shrimp, chicken, and eggs in a "gravy" with many vegetables and seasonings

Lily's Wai Sek Hong

Chef Lily Ng

www.lilyng2000.blogspot.com

Chef Lily Ng

Lily's Wai Sek Hong is a popular food blog administered by Lily Ng, a stay-at-home grandmother in Aurora, Colorado, who taught herself to cook and bake from cookbooks and by watching cooking programs on television.

About Ketchup

Many people don't realize that this seemingly all-American condiment actually has its origins in Asia. It consisted of a base of pickled fish brine to which other spices were added. The sweet yet tangy tomato kind we're familiar with today came later. It was originally sold by farmers and, in the 1800s when people were uncertain about the safety of eating raw tomatoes, this was the preferred method of consuming them. Today, Heinz, one of the largest producers of ketchup, sells 650 million bottles annually around the world. In Asian dishes, as in other cuisines, it is most often used as a condiment or to make sauces.

Serves 6

For Mee Bandung Gravy:
3 qt/3 L water
¼ lb/100 g shallots, peeled and sliced
2 oz/60 g garlic, peeled and sliced
3 oz/90 g Chinese celery, sliced
¼ 1b/100 g ripe tomatoes, sliced
3 oz/80 g ginger, crushed
1½ oz/40 g beef bouillion
1½ oz/50 g prawn cube
1 cup/200 g tomato ketchup
1½ oz/45 g chili boh
¼ cup/50 g sugar
1 egg white

3½ lb/1.6 kg yellow noodles
3 fish cakes, sliced
4 cups/400 g bean sprouts, blanched
½ lb/250 g cooked chicken, shredded
½ lb/200 g prawns, cooked and peeled
3 hard boiled eggs, cut into quarters

Garnish:
½ cup/40 g green onions, sliced
¼ cup/40 g Chinese celery, sliced
1 oz/30 g red chilies, sliced
¼ cup/50 g shallots, sliced and fried
10 key limes (calamansi will be better)
½ cup/100 g roasted peanuts, ground

1. Put water in a large pot and bring to a boil. Add in sliced shallots, garlic, celery, tomatoes, and crushed ginger. Reduce to low heat and simmer for 3-5 minutes.

2. Add beef bouillon, prawn cube, tomato ketchup and chilli boh. Stir well and adjust seasoning with sugar to taste.

3. Simmer for 5 minutes and strain.

4. Put gravy back on the stove and gradually add in beaten egg white. Remove pot from stove but keep it warm.

1. Blanch yellow noodles in a pot of boiling water for a few seconds.

2. Remove, strain and place it into serving bowls.

3. Add in sliced fish cake and blanched bean sprouts.

4. Pour in hot Bandung gravy and top with shredded chicken, prawns, and boiled egss. Garnish with green onions, celery, chilies, fried shallots, and calamansi.

5. Sprinkle with ground peanuts and serve hot.

NAAM NIEOW

For this noodle stall version of a popular Asian dish, there are no set ingredient amounts—play around with the proportions to find what suits your taste buds

Servings vary

For the Soup:

Pork ribs and bones

Pork blood

Dry kapok flowers

Water

Boil everything together and
keep it hot in soup pot.

Chinese flat egg noodles (khanom jeen--looks
    very much like fettuccine)

For Paste 1:

Dried red chilies

Dried fermented soy beans

Shallots

Garlic

Shrimp paste

Salt

Pound all ingredients together until well mixed
    and a paste forms.

Chef Paa (Aunty) Yaa

Born on the Burmese side of the Golden
Triangle fifty-something years ago, Pa Yaa was
a farmer's daughter, growing enough for the
family and selling any excess they could in the
markets of Mae Sai, the biggest border town in
the area. It was on one of these selling missions
that she met her Thai husband, Lung Suk. They
married twenty years ago and the family moved
to Sob Ruak. Her aunt set up a stall selling Nam
Ngieow noodles and Pa Yaa had a business
alongside, selling deep fried bananas, a favorite
local desert. When her aunt retired, Pa Yaa took
over the whole business and continues cooking
traditional cuisine that is much loved in her area.

For Paste 2:

Minced pork or fish meat (catfish or snake fish)

Onions, chopped

Garlic, chopped

Tomatoes, chopped

1. Boil minced pork/minced fish meat until soft.

2. Add onions and fry in vegetable oil until fragrant.

3. Add garlic and fry until it turns yellow.

4. Add the tomatoes and stir-fry until meat is done.

Condiments:

Fresh spring onions and fresh coriander leaves (cut in
    small pieces)

Pickled cabbages (sliced)

Bean sprouts and sliced fresh cabbages (or any
    available fresh vegetables)

Lime juice/vinegar

Chili powder

Fish sauce (or soy sauce)

Sugar

1. Soak noodles in hot water for 20 seconds (just to
    make them soft), and put them in a bowl.

2. Add some of both pastes.

3. Pour in hot soup (with bones and kapok flowers).

4. Put pickled cabbages, chopped spring onion, and
    coriander leaves on top.

5. Serve vegetables and other condiments on the
    side, and let each person add to taste.

PANCIT CANTON

Stir-fried egg noodles with Chinese sausage and chicken

Kuma Inn

113 Ludlow St. 2nd Floor
New York, NY 10002
(212) 353-8866

Cuisine: Filipino, Thai, and Southeast Asian

Chef King Phojanakong

Located in the heart of New York's
Lower East Side, Kuma Inn is a cozy
restaurant tucked away on the second
floor, serving tasty small plates at a
reasonable price.

Serves 4-6

3 tbsp canola oil

1 tbsp garlic, chopped

⅓ cup/53 g onions, sliced

1 link Chinese style sausage, sliced

6 oz/170 g raw chicken breast, sliced

⅓ cup/50 g carrots, julienned

⅓ cup/35 g bean sprouts

1 cup/60 g bok choy, sliced

4 cups/225 g egg noodles, par cooked

½ cup/120 ml water or chicken stock

2 tbsp fish sauce, or to taste

2 tbsp oyster sauce, or to taste

Black pepper, to taste

Scallions, sliced and lime wedge to garnish

1. Heat oil in wok or pan. Sauté garlic, onions, sausage, chicken, carrots, bean sprouts, and bok choy until chicken is cooked through.

2. Add noodles and sauté.

3. Season by adding water or chicken stock, fish sauce, oyster sauce, and black pepper. Sauté briefly.

4. Garnish with scallions and lime wedges.

King Phojanakong

Phojanakong is chef-owner of two NYC restaurants, Kuma Inn in Manhattan's Lower East Side and Umi Nom in Bed-Stuy, Brooklyn. King is a born-and-bred New Yorker whose culinary influences began at home with the inspirational cooking of his Filipino mother and Thai father. Spending summers in the Philippines throughout his childhood furthered his interest in the culinary world and instilled in him the importance of community and culture.

PHOENIX AND DRAGON OVER NOODLE PANCAKE

A traditional shrimp and chicken dish

M.Y. CHINA

M.Y. China
845 Market Street, Level 4
San Francisco, CA 94103
(415) 580-3001

Cuisine: Chinese

Chef Martin Yan

M.Y. China offers authentic Chinese cuisine in a modern experience. Inspired by Chef Martin Yan and his years of teaching the art of Chinese cuisine, a full exhibition kitchen brings the ancient art of the wok, hand-pulled noodles, and dim sum to light.

Serves 4

For the Pancake:

6 oz/170 g fresh egg noodles

1 tbsp vegetable oil

1. To make the pancake: Preheat oven to 200°F/95°C.

2. Bring a large pot of salted water to a boil. Cook noodles according to package directions. Drain.

3. Heat half of the oil in a large nonstick skillet over medium heat. Add noodles, flattening out to an even layer, and cook until golden brown, 3-5 minutes.

4. Flip pancake and drizzle remaining oil around the pan and continue to cook until second side is browned and crisp, 2-4 minutes. Keep pancake warm in oven.

Chef Martin Yan

The celebrated host of over 3,000 cooking shows broadcast worldwide, Martin Yan enjoys distinction as a certified Master Chef, a highly respected food consultant, a cooking instructor, and a prolific author.

For the Phoenix and Dragon:

2 tbsp cornstarch

4 tbsp Chinese rice wine

Salt

½ lb/230 g medium raw shrimp, shelled and deveined, leaving tails intact

6 oz/170 g boneless, skinless chicken breast, cut into strips

½ cup/120 ml chicken broth

1½ tsp sesame oil

1 tsp soy sauce

1 tsp sugar

Salt and ground white pepper

2 tbsp vegetable oil

1 tbsp minced garlic

1 tsp minced ginger

¼ red bell pepper, cut into 1-inch pieces

½ cup/35 g snow peas, halved

Cornstarch solution (1 tsp cornstarch dissolved in 2 tsp water)

1. For Phoenix and Dragon: Mix 1 tbsp cornstarch, 2 tbsp wine, and a pinch of salt in a bowl. Add shrimp. Mix 1 tbsp cornstarch, 2 tbsp wine, and a pinch of salt in a second bowl. Add chicken. Set both aside to let marinate for 10 minutes.

2. Make the sauce by combining chicken broth, sesame oil, soy sauce, sugar, and salt and pepper to taste. Set aside.

3. Heat a wok over high heat. Add 2 tbsp oil, swirling to coat sides. Add garlic and ginger and cook until fragrant, 5 seconds.

4. Add shrimp and chicken and stir-fry until just cooked through, about 1 minute.

5. Add bell pepper, snow peas, and sauce and bring to a boil. Add cornstarch solution and stir until sauce thickens.

6. Place noodle pancake on a platter and top with the chicken and shrimp stir-fry. Serve immediately.

PORK NOODLE LAKSA WITH SHRIMP

The "noodles" are made from pork skin and served with a curry spiced sauce

Phat Thai

343 Main Street
Carbondale, CO 81623
(970) 963-7001

Cuisine: Thai-inspired

Chef Mark Fischer

Phat Thai isn't a traditional Thai restaurant. It isn't even Thai—or even Asian. It doesn't attempt to create a fusion or copy provincial classics. It is inspired by Thai cuisine and how that makes Chef Fischer feel!

Chef Mark Fischer

When Fischer moved to Boulder to go to college, he planned to become a doctor. But while tending bar as a student, he became interested in the food industry. Returning to his native Pittsburgh, he enrolled in cooking school. On a skiing trip to Aspen after graduation, he decided to open Six89 in Carbondale, and then subsequently, a Southeast Asian restaurant named Phat Thai down the street. Next, he opened The Pullman in Glenwood Springs, and most recently, Phat Thai, a larger version of his Carbondale restaurant with the same name. Fischer is also an avid mountain biker.

Pork Noodles

4lb/2kg pork skin, fresh or frozen

1 tbsp baking soda

2 tbsp kosher salt

1. In a large pot, cover the pork with water. Add baking soda and salt and bring to a boil. Reduce to a simmer and cook for 90 minutes or until tender. Skim off any scum that floats to the surface.

2. Drain well. Then, while the skin is still warm and pliable, scrape any fat from the underside of the skin. It will be tender, so finesse is required. Some tears and rips are inevitable.

3. After all the skin has been cleaned, julienne approximately ⅛ inch/3 mm wide and reserve. (You should have approximately 8 cups/2 L of noodles.)

Serves 8

For the Dish:

2 tbsp blended oil

2 tbsp Thai chilies, minced

2 tbsp garlic minced

½ cup/100 g palm sugar (or brown sugar)

2 tbsp yellow curry powder—Malaysian

2 tbsp yellow curry paste

32 shrimp, peeled and deveined, head on preferably

48 oz/1.5 L coconut milk

1 cup/240 ml vegetable stock

Pork noodles (reserved from recipe at left)

1 cup/170 g red chilies, julienned fine

2 lemongrass stalks, peeled, trimmed, and shaved
    thinly crosswise

8 kaffir lime leaves, stemmed and julienned

3 cups/265 g bok choy, coarsely chopped

½ cup/120 ml fish sauce

Garnish:

Toasted cashews

Toasted coconut

Cilantro

1. In a large, shallow pot, over high heat, heat oil until it shimmers. Add Thai chilies and garlic, stirring constantly.

2. As soon as they become aromatic, add sugar, curry powder, and curry paste. Continue stirring until it, too, becomes aromatic.

3. Add shrimp and toss to coat.

4. Add coconut milk and vegetable stock. Bring to a simmer.

5. Add pork noodles and return to a simmer.

6. Add red chilies, lemongrass, lime leaf, and bok choy.

7. Adjust the seasonings with fish sauce.

8. Divide the laska evenly between eight deep bowls.

9. Garnish each with toasted coconut, cashews, and cilantro.

SINGAPORE MEI FUN NOODLES

Shrimp, chicken, and lots of veggies come together in this quick noodle dish

ASIAN BISTRO & NIGHTCLUB

TAO

42 E. 58th Street
New York, NY 10022
(212) 888-2288

Also a location in Las Vegas, Nevada

Cuisine: Japanese

Chef Ralph Scamardella

Originally a nineteenth-century stable for the Vanderbilt family, and then a balconied movie theater, TAO NY was transformed into a majestic Asian "temple."

Serves 2

4 oz /113 g thin rice noodles, dry,
    soaked in water
⅛ cup/30 ml blended oil
2 oz/60 g shredded carrots
2 oz/60 g sliced shiitake mushrooms
2 oz/60 g sliced snow peas
2 oz/60 g sliced red onions
1 oz/30 g sliced red pepper
1 oz/30 g sliced yellow pepper
¼ tsp chopped garlic
1 tbsp yellow curry powder
1 tsp salt
1 tsp sugar
3 oz/90 g blanched shrimp, 41-50 count
3 oz/90 g cooked chicken

1. Blanch the noodles in boiling water
   and drain.

2. Heat oil in a wok.

3. Add all vegetables and sauté about
   5 minutes.

4. Add garlic and toss.

5. Stir in curry, salt and sugar.

6. Add noodles, shrimp, and chicken.
   Sauté until shrimp is cooked.

7. Adjust seasonings and serve.

About Curry

While many people think of curry as a spice,
it is really a blend of several spices. There are
many kinds of curry, but most will contain
some combination of chilies (the heat factor),
turmeric (where the yellow color comes from),
coriander, and cumin. To this base of spices
can be added any or all of the following:
ginger, garlic, fennel seed, caraway, cinnamon,
clove, mustard seed, green or black cardamom,
nutmeg, and black pepper. Experiment with
your own combination.

SMOKED CHICKEN WITH LACQUERED BACON, CABBAGE, AND PICKLED CARROTS AND DAIKON

This noodle recipe incorporates the chef's love of BBQ by combining smoked chicken and bacon with Asian spices

Brother Jimmy's

1485 2nd Avenue
New York, NY 10075
(212) 426-2020

Cuisine: North Carolina barbecue

Chef Eva Pesantez

Brother Jimmy's motto is: "Put Some South in Yo' Mouth." Anyone looking for great Southern food set to a blues, rock 'n' roll and country soundtrack knows to head through its doors.

Chef Eva Pesantez

Eva Pesantez's passion for food and natural culinary acumen has been the driving force in her success in the food industry. Currently the Corporate Executive Chef for all Brother Jimmy's locations, Eva has used her experience, skills, and instinct to elevate the cuisine at the always popular NYC BBQ restaurants.

About Chinese Five-Spice Powder

Legend has it that the ancient Chinese wanted to create a "wonder powder" that encompassed the five Elements: Wood, Fire, Earth, Metal, and Water. Traditionally, five-spice powder is a blend of fennel, cloves, cinnamon, star anise, and peppercorns and so offers the five flavors of sour, bitter, sweet, pungent and salty all at the same time. This seasoning contributes a distinctive taste and flavorful balance to any dish.

Serves 4-6

For the Smoked Chicken Legs:

2 tsp five-spice powder

1 tsp ground black pepper

1½ tsp granulated sugar

1½ tsp kosher salt

1½ tbsp apple wood chips

2 large chicken legs/thighs

For the Pickled Daikon and Carrots:

1 cup/150 g daikon, cut into long matchsticks

1 cup/150 g carrot, cut into long matchsticks

¼ cup + 2 tsp granulated sugar

1½ tsp kosher salt

½ cup120 ml rice wine vinegar

¼ cup/60 ml boiling water

Place the julienned daikon and carrots in a bowl with 2 teaspoons of sugar and 1 teaspoon of salt. Mix well several times for 3 minutes until the sticks are bendable. Rinse and let drain well. In a nonreactive or glass bowl mix hot water with the remaining sugar and salt until dissolved. Add the daikon and carrots, mix well and allow to cool, then refrigerate.

For the Sauce:

2 tbsp hoisin sauce

2 tbsp Shaoxing wine

2 tbsp soy sauce – I prefer low sodium

2 tbsp granulated sugar

1 tbsp rice vinegar

1 tbsp grated ginger

¼ cup/60 ml water

For the Udon:

1 lb/450 g fresh udon noodles

2 tbsp canola oil

½ large Spanish onion, sliced about ¼ inch thick

4 green onions, thick green part sliced on the bias

2 cups/680 g thin sliced savoy cabbage

3 slices apple wood smoked bacon, julienned

1 cup/60 g sugar snap peas, sliced on a bias

Toss the smoked chicken legs, pickled daikon and carrots, udon noodles, and sauce, and mix well.

Smoked chicken legs, see page 274. Can be done the day before.

SMOKED CHICKEN LEGS

If you don't want to go through the process of smoking your own chicken (though I think it is worth it!) you may purchase smoked chicken or duck legs—though with duck legs you might need 4.

2 tsp five-spice powder

1 tsp ground black pepper

1½ tsp granulated sugar

1½ tsp kosher salt

1½ tbsp apple wood chips

2 large chicken legs/thighs

1. Combine the spices and rub all over the legs including under the skin. Refrigerate and let sit for at least 4 hours. When you are ready to smoke them, remove from the refrigerator and let sit out for 30 minutes, then smoke.

2. Set your smoker according to the manufacturer's instructions. Line the drip tray with foil for an easier cleanup. Place the apple chips on the bottom of the smoker and then set up with the drip pan and rack. Place the legs on the rack so they are not touching. Turn the flame on to medium, and as soon as the chips start smoking cover the smoker and cook for about 30 minutes until the legs have an internal temperature of 170°F/77° C.

3. When the chicken legs are finished, let them sit for 10-15 minutes to cool slightly. Remove the skin and discard, then pull the meat from the bone. Shred the larger pieces into thinner strips, being careful not to include any thin bones or gristle in with the meat. Set aside.

About Smoked Chicken Legs

These can be made at home with a stovetop smoker, which is easy to use and is not dependent on the weather. Stovetop smoking imparts a smoky flavor faster than outdoor smoking, and so the smoking time will be shorter. There is a wide variety of flavors available, depending on the type of wood you choose. In addition to apple, used here, cherry, hickory, pecan, and mesquite are a few other options that will each result in a distinctly different taste.

TAN TAN NOODLE SOUP

Tan Tan Noodles take their name from the carrying pole used by vendors who would roam
the city offering the dish to sweltering citizens in need of a good lunch—and a good sweat

ChongQing

2808 Commercial Drive
Vancouver, B.C.
Canada V5N 4C6
(604) 254-7434

Two other locations,
one in Vancouver
and another in Burnaby

Cuisine: Szechuanese

Chef Paul Zhang

Chef Paul Zhang's pioneering ChongQing
Restaurant has been Vancouver's go-to
destination for hot and spicy Szechuan
noodles for over two decades. His menu
pays homage to the central Chinese city of
ChonQing, known for its hot summers during
which residents gorge on spicy food to induce
sweating and lower body temperatures. Paul's
signature specialty is Tan Tan Noodles.

Serves 2

2 cups canola oil

½ cup/60 g paprika

½ cup/60 g ground chili powder

½ cup/90 g peanut butter

½ tbsp dried shrimp, diced

½ tbsp preserved vegetable (ja choy)

Vinegar

Sesame oil

2 cups/475 ml chicken stock

1 lb/500 g cooked ramen noodles

Chopped green onions (for garnish)

1. Bring canola oil to a boil. Remove from heat and stir in paprika and chili powder. Let mixture sit overnight.

2. Mix peanut butter and ⅓ cup of hot oil mixture (only take the oil and not the residue of paprika and chili powder on bottom of mixture) till smooth.

3. Then mix in dried shrimp and preserved vegetable (ja choy). Add a splash of vinegar and a splash of sesame oil.

5. Bring stock to a boil. Add peanut butter mixture and stir to combine.

6. Add cooked ramen noodles to soup. Pour into bowls and garnish with scallions.

Chef Paul Zhang

From an early age, Zhang knew the importance of quality food. He is the third generation of chef/restauranteurs in his family. Zhang has expanded the family business to three successful restaurants throughout Greater Vancouver.

About Ja Choy

This preserved vegetable is the knobby stem of the mustard plant that is pickled. The process is similar to Korean kimchi: The stem is pressed, salted, and dried, then rubbed with hot red chili paste and left to ferment in an earthenware jar. Like cucumber pickles, they are crunchy but tender and can be sweet, sour, or spicy depending on the region and preparation. You may find it in the store under a number of fun-to-say names: cha tsai, tsa tsai, jar choy, jar choi, ja choi, ja choy, or cha tsoi.

TOM YUM PORK NOODLE SOUP

The taste of this pork and fish soup can be tailored to suit your taste by varying the amounts of the seasonings

SriPraPhai
See-Pra-Pie
Thai Restaurant

SriPraPhai

64-13 39th Avenue
Woodside, NY 11377
(718) 899-9599

Cuisine: Thai

Chef Sripraphai Tipmanee

SriPraPhai has been the top Zagat-rated Thai restaurant in NYC for nine straight years.

About Peanuts

China is the leading producer of peanuts in the world, with a share of over 40%. This probably accounts for their popularity as an ingredient and garnish in many Asian dishes. This is a relatively recent development, however, as peanuts were not introduced to China until the seventeenth century and production didn't really take off until the 1980s. In addition to providing crunch and flavor to dishes, peanuts are nutritional powerhouses containing a whopping 25% protein (the highest percentage of any tree nut) and having a high antioxidant content as well.

Serves 4

2 tbsp soy sauce

2 tbsp tapioca flour

1 tsp pepper

½ cup/120 ml water

1 cup/230 g sliced pork

1 cup/220 g ground pork

8 cups/2 L broth (soup)

1 lb/450 g dried rice noodles, soaked until
    softened

2 cups/200 g bean sprouts

8 fish balls

8 fried fish balls

½ cup/120 ml soy sauce

½ cup/100 g sugar

⅓ cup/80 ml lime juice

¼ cup/40 g ground peanuts

2 tsp chili powder

Garnish:

Bean sprouts

Lime slices

¼ cup/15 g chopped green onions

¼ cup/8 g chopped cilantro

¼ cup/40 g fried garlic

Chef Sripraphai Tipmanee

Tipmanee arrived in New York thirty-eight years ago and began working as a nurse. She subsequently started an electrical appliance store catering to Thai students who shipped American-branded goods and appliances home to Thailand. When American companies started selling their products directly in Thailand, Tipmanee converted the store into a bakery. As her Thai and other customer base grew, she expanded the bakery into SriPraPhai restaurant. The original menu had only four or five selections. Over the years this has grown to over 120 dishes representing every region of Thailand.

1. Mix soy sauce, tapioca flour, pepper, and water and put both kinds of pork in to marinate.

2. Heat a pot of water to boiling and heat the broth to boiling in another pot.

3. Put the rice noodles and bean sprouts into boiling water for about 15-20 seconds, then put into serving bowls.

4. Boil the fish balls and fried fish ball for about 30 seconds and divide among the same bowls.

5. Put the ground pork and sliced pork in the pot of broth to cook. Then add soy sauce, sugar, and lime juice.

4. Pour the pork soup into the serving bowls with the noodles. Then add peanuts and chili.

5. Garnish with fresh bean sprouts, slice of lime, green onions, cilantro, and garlic.

WAGYU BEEF SATE NOODLES

A beef noodle dish flavored with dried shrimp and peanut butter

Starry Kitchen Nights @ Tiara Cafe

127 E. 9th Street
Los Angeles, CA 90015
(213) 814-1123

Cuisine: Eclectic

Chef Thi Tran

The launch of Starry Kitchen debuted in Tran's and husband Nyuyen Tran's North Hollywood apartment, serving lunch for a modest $5 suggested donation. After a couple of interesting moves along the way, Starry Kitchen is now a dinner-only restaurant located inside Fred Eric's Tiara Cafe.

Chef Thi Tran

Tran was born to a Chinese family in Vietnam, but was raised in Dallas.

Serves 3-4

3 stalks lemongrass, minced
    (use white part only)

7 cloves of garlic, minced

1 cup/75 g dried shrimp
    (soaked in water until softened, then
    minced by hand or food processor)

5 cups/1.2 L chicken broth
    (canned or homemade)

1½ cups/350 ml of sate sauce
    (may also be called barbecue sauce in
    Asian grocery stores)

1 can coconut soda

3 heaping tbsp crunchy peanut butter

2½ cups/600 ml water

1 tbsp lee kum kee chicken bouillon

5 oz/140 g fresh rice stick noodles or your
    choice of noodles

5 thin slices wagyu beef or rib eye, lightly seared

1. Make sate sauce: Heat up wok/pan and sauté lemongrass until fragrant.

2. Lower heat and add garlic and dried shrimp.

4. Add chicken broth, sate, coconut soda, peanut butter, water, and chicken bouillon.

5. Cook noodles according to package directions and place in serving bowls.

6. Place beef on top and pour sate sauce over all.

Garnish as desired with: shredded romaine lettuce, thin slices of tomatoes, julienne cucumbers, anise basil, and Tia To or Vietnamese perilla, along with a side of finely sliced Thai Chili and a quarter lime wedge, to be squeezed on top of the noodles before mixing.

About Wagyu Beef

The literal translation of Wagyu is Japanese Cow. The breeds of cattle that fall into this category are genetically predisposed to have meat that is intensely marbleized and have a high percentage of unsaturated fat as well as a higher percentage of Omega-3 fatty acids. It is highly valued. Wagyu cattle also enjoy beer and sake, which is sometimes added to their diet, although it is not thought to have any effect on the flavor of the meat.

INDEX